CALAIS: ME

BOOK TWO

RICHARD FOREMAN

Copyright © 2025 by Richard Foreman

The right of R. Foreman to be identified as the author of this work has been asserted by him in accordance with the Copyright, Designs and Patents Act, 1988.

First published in 2025 by Sharpe Books.

CALAIS

1.

"Slit their throats while they're asleep. Torch the house and turn their bones to ash. Just ensure that no one survives, and hell is filled even more to the rafters," Raymon Creton, the French spymaster, had remarked to Arnaud Bernier. "I am even tempted to come with you, to ensure the job is done properly. And Grey is dead."

Bernier doubted that the spy was being sincere. Creton was known for using others to carry out his dirty work. The official was not devoid of malice, but he was short on physical courage. Years ago, Creton had employed the former soldier to lead coastal raids against the English. Bernier was happy to do so again. For the right price.

The middle-aged Breton, with lank black hair framing a gnarled countenance, wore a mail coat that had seen better days. A dagger hung from his belt. The leather was cracked and crusted with mud. Rings were rusty or missing. He told himself he would buy a new one when he could. The great pestilence had not been good for business. Peace hadn't been good for business. His stomach churned from the remnants of seasickness rather than from an uneasy conscience. Bernier had promised himself, as a young soldier, that he would never murder a woman in cold blood. But promises are meant to be broken. No deed was too wicked if the money was good. Mercenaries are mercenary, after all.

It was the dead of night, as cold as a crypt. The perfect time to attack. Kill. Bernier could still taste the salt in the gelid air. If he concentrated, the Frenchman could probably still hear the waves crash against the cliffs of the south coast, see tufts of foam in the Stygian waters. But his focus was on the cottage before him. It was time. The agent, who just went by the name Colban, that Creton had sent ahead to gather intelligence, had informed him that their principal target, Sir Hugh Grey, was in the house - along with the man-at-arms, the French woman and her maid.

Bernier was armed with a crossbow. A quarrel lay along its spine, waiting to be unleashed. He commenced to come out from the blackberry bushes and shrubbery at the end of the garden and made his way towards the thatched dwelling. Skeletal fruit trees hung over the lawn. The Frenchman observed a nearby vegetable patch and pens on the grounds, which were now empty of livestock. During the worst of the pestilence the Englishman had sought to make his household more self-sufficient, no doubt. Bernier could also observe the outline of a row of make-shift crosses, marking graves. Death was everyone's bedfellow these past couple of years. There were rumours that a third of Christendom had perished. His own village numbers had been halved by the dreaded boil. The property was remote, which may have been a blessing against the contagion - but it now made the house vulnerable to attack. No one would hear the prospective screams or cries for help. Creton had been right. "You will come and go before anyone can raise the alarm. The tide will be coming in when you land and be going out when you depart."

Heavy boots crunched upon the frost covered grass. To the left of Bernier was Colban, a wolfish grin animating his swarthy complexion. Thankfully, he could (just about) understand the Scot when he gave his report. Colban was perhaps picturing the Frenchwoman and her maid. The fair creatures were fair game in the agent's mind. Spoils of war. On the other side of Bernier was his second-in-command, Jean Roet, still somewhat green behind the gills from the crossing. The pot-bellied, bearded ex-soldier looked like he had just been sick, or was about to vomit. He may also have appeared out of sorts after hearing that his cut from the raid wouldn't be as substantial as he initially hoped. He would look to secure some booty from the house as compensation. The Frenchwoman hopefully possessed some jewellery, the English aristocrat some coin. Roet would have frightened many a soul, even in daylight. Black fingernails. Blacker teeth. An even blacker heart. The veteran clutched the crucifix around his neck for good luck, a small ritual he conducted just before setting himself to kill, before retrieving his axe.

At the rear of the cottage another brace of Frenchmen - Pierre and Guiscard - advanced, armed with short swords. The bald-headed brothers with almost comically bushy eyebrows would enter through the backdoor and prevent any of their prey from fleeing. They swayed a little, as if tipsy, as they made their way through the whistling iron gate. The captain of their small vessel had said that the wind and crossing would be fair. But the brothers had still to fully regain their land legs.

Bernier scowled at the creaking stairs after making his way through the front door, which had been blessingly unsecured. The Frenchman led his companions up to the first floor of the cottage and its three bedrooms. He would take the room to his far left, believing it to be the largest and the chamber containing the English spymaster. He stepped forward across the landing as stealthily as possible, turning back and nodding to his confederates to each enter the remaining rooms. Despite the chill in the air his palms grew sweaty.

The crossbow weighed heavy in his right hand as he opened the warped wooden door with his left and entered. A smell of perfume suffused in the air. Bernier realised that the large room, which ran along the entire left side of the property, belonged to the Frenchwoman - the daughter of the traitor Michiel Auclair. Embers glowed in the fireplace. A curtain billowed from a breeze exhaling through a gap in the windowpane. There were some pictures on the wall, pieces of furniture and items of clothing spread throughout the room. The assassin rightly concentrated on the bulge in the bed at the far side of the chamber, taking a couple of steps forward as he did so.

Bernier couched the deadly weapon in his shoulder, took a breath and fired. A slight twang was swiftly succeeded by the sound of the crossbow bolt striking the lump on the bed. But something was wrong. The sound wasn't right.

The mercenary's baffled expression quickly turned to one of shock - and agony - as the English man-at-arms appeared from behind the door, unsheathed his enemy's dagger and plunged the blade into his stubbled throat, puncturing any scream. The soldier never enjoyed killing, but the look of satisfaction on his face understandably eclipsed that on his victim's countenance.

William Gower had been awake when Bernier and his men advanced across the frosted lawn. He had been asking himself the question again. Should he try and make an honest woman of the figure sleeping next to him? Was there such thing as an honest man? Gower had made a vow to Eleanor - and God - that he would remain faithful to her. He had no desire to turn any wife into a widow, however. The great pestilence was receding. But the war would soon resume as a result. He was a soldier - and soldiers fought. Gower was too proud to live off Eleanor's inheritance.

"You are good for her, William. And Eleanor deserves to have good things in her life," his employer had argued.

"Does she not deserve to marry someone noble?"

Sir Hugh Grey here laughed, before replying:

"You're far nobler, William, than a tournament full of knights. You may not realise it, but Eleanor does, I warrant."

He loved her dearly. They made each another laugh. Why shouldn't he propose?

Before Gower had an opportunity to answer the question he was distracted by the encroaching spectral figures. He woke Eleanor up. Despite her drowsiness and confusion, she duly followed his instructions and concealed herself behind a number of dresses hanging in a closet, whilst Gower placed the pillows on the bed beneath the sheets, to give the impression that someone was still sleeping there, before positioning himself behind the door. Dressed in breeches and a nightshirt, the soldier felt slightly naked without a sword in his hand, but he did not want to retreat to his room and leave Eleanor. Gower was tall and as powerfully built as an archer. A fringe of black curls covered a scar on his forehead. His expression could be friendly, especially when cradling a cup of ale, but his face appeared anything but welcoming now.

Jean Roet entered the middle room, squinting in the gloom. A large portrait hung over a rosewood desk, of the aristocrat's wife and daughter - who had been murdered several years ago by Frenchmen during a raid. The room was also home to several shelves, weighed down with all manner of books. Roet's knuckles turned white as he gripped the handaxe he was carrying. The bed was empty but a door to an adjoining room was open. Could his quarry be in there? The mercenary had never hacked a man to death before while his victim was sitting over a chamber pot. But he would be willing to.

The Scotsman initially feasted his eyes upon the door, perhaps picturing the woman behind it. Colban had kept watch over the house earlier, to make sure Grey, his bodyguard and the daughter of the French traitor were present. He had grown lusty-eyed and licked his lips, feeling a familiar itch in his groin (which wasn't the pox), at observing the fine figure of a woman. The room was smaller than the Scot expected and spartanly furnished. Colban pursed his lips and grunted, realising that he was in the bodyguard's quarters. A hunting bow and polished broadsword hung on the wall. The man-at-arms was absent, however. Where was he? Could he have left the house without being noticed? The Scotsman failed to imagine that the lowly soldier might be sharing the same bed as the refined Frenchwoman.

As was his habit, Sir Hugh Grey was at work in his small study at the back of the house, next to the maid's room. A solitary candle burned on a table, as the spymaster worked his way through a mound of correspondence, composing letters to dignitaries, agents, friends and business associates. He was pleased that his agent in Florence had uncovered some compromising material on one of the king's creditors. Grey could now use the intelligence to leverage a delay in the treasury paying back the loan or receive a more favourable rate of interest.

His ears twitched as he heard a noise. They further twitched soon after, recognising French voices as Pierre shoved open the stiff back entrance to the cottage. The nobleman remained calm. He appeared mildly irked rather than surprised or distressed. As the whispering voices and footsteps grew louder Grey picked up the knife which lay on his plate - which he had used to cut some cheese and fruit with - and disappeared into a blind spot at the entrance to his study. The intruders would have to pass him to get to Constance's quarters. The maid would be fast asleep, no doubt. Hopefully Gower would stir in time. He worried for Eleanor - and Constance - more than for himself. Indeed, the thought of death often brought the widower solace. He would see his wife and daughter again. Grace and Beatrice. Although such had been his sins since their deaths it was likely that he would be sent to the other place.

Sir Hugh Grey wore a dark woollen coat over an embroidered shirt. He possessed sharp features and a sharper mind. The spymaster had the king's ear. Rivals at court would comment that Grey held too much sway over Edward, arguing that the widower's desire for revenge had spurred the English monarch on to claim the French crown.

The usually sanguine, or stoical, spy felt his heartbeat quicken as the French intruders approached Constance's door. Unfortunately, at least one of the intruders would see him when he appeared from out of the nook of his study. He needed a distraction. But it was now or never.

The only thing Gower knew about the men who had entered the house was that he wanted to kill them. Blood marked his forearm and spotted his face as he came out of the bedroom and glowered at Jean Roet, who was somewhat disconcerted to see the fearsome Englishman, as opposed to Bernier, standing before him in the glow of an overhanging oil lamp.

"I need help," the Frenchman blurted out in his native language, not a little distressed, calling for his companions.

Gower purposefully strode towards Roet, holding Bernier's dagger aloft. Whilst the intruder was momentarily transfixed by the blade in the Englishman's right-hand, Gower used his left to deliver a powerful punch, which almost dislocated his opponent's jaw. The man-at-arms then wasted little time in jabbing his weapon into Roet's left eye socket.

The Scotsman came onto the landing and stood at the top of the stairs and spat out a garbled curse. Roet lay on the floor, his right leg twitching. All but dead. It was likely that that Bernier had been killed too. The agent was still determined to complete his mission, however. He had willingly accepted Creton's assignment. He had agreed to join the attack on the house, as opposed to just reconnoitre the property - and not just because of the extra money on offer. Due to the truce, it had been some time since the Scot had drawn English blood. Surely the brothers were still downstairs and would join him shortly, he thought. Hoped.

Gower picked up the axe from the floor and strode towards the enemy, his face a picture of cold, murderous intent. He would let his opponent attack first, Make his first - and last - mistake. Colban thrust his sword forward. But the man-at-arms deftly moved to the side and in a swift, fluid movement brought the axe down on the intruder's hand, scything through fingers, webbing and the Scotsman's wrist - causing him to drop his blade. Colban took a couple of steps backwards, but he was cornered. Damned. Gower had vowed to protect Eleanor, as well as remain faithful to her. The agent held his trembling hands aloft.

"Do you accept my surrender?"

"No," the Englishman replied, dismissively, before burying the axe head in the man's chest and lungs. The Scot emitted a gargling noise and then perished.

Gower observed the silhouette of Grey at the bottom of the stairs. Blood dripped from his knife. When the brothers had turned their attention to the raised voices on the first floor the spy made his move - it was now or never - and calmly and surgically stabbed both mercenaries in the back of the head. The attack was quick but hopefully not painless. They fell to the floor, like puppets with their strings cut. The more Frenchmen the widower killed, the more likely it was that he would be murdering the villains who had butchered his wife and daughter.

"Do you know who is behind this?" Gower asked, his blood up, thinking how the spymaster had made his share of enemies, foreign and domestic, over the years.

"Yes. And I know what to do about it," Sir Hugh Grey replied, his tone as chilling as the night air.

2.

Midday.

The frost had thawed. But the sun still seemed distant, sterile, when it wasn't retreating behind dirty grey clouds. A mist hung on the horizon, though one could still just about observe the church spire over the tops of the trees.

The two men rode on, already tired and weary. At first light, after enduring a sleepless night, the household packed necessities and valuables and travelled to the estate of Sir Walter Harewell, a local landowner. Grey asked his fellow aristocrat to take in Eleanor and her maid, explaining that he had to venture to London by order of the king. Either out of fear of Grey, or a love for his wife, Sir Walter would not bother his guests with any untoward advances. They would be well looked after. Sir Walter also possessed a small retinue of former soldiers who guarded the house and patrolled the land to ward of poachers.

"What will you do when you find the people responsible for the attack?" Constance asked her master, perhaps already knowing the answer.

"It's doubtful that we'll buy them a Christmas present," Grey drily replied, whilst saddling his horse, Penelope.

The spymaster recalled the report from one of his agents in Paris. Creton had boasted that he was intent on uncovering the whereabouts of Sir Hugh Grey. "My aim is to remove the significant piece from the board before we re-commence the game." Grey had briefly turned his mind to who could have betrayed him. Either no one name or too many came to mind. It's a spy's fate to make as many enemies as allies. Perhaps he could extract the traitor's identity from Creton. It would be his dying words.

The once fecund Cornish landscape appeared desolate, and not just because they were in the bowels of winter. England was a far from green and pleasant land. A plume of smoke spiralled upwards, perhaps from a cremation pit. Grey recalled the unholy and unbearable stench from the burning of the dead in the capital, during the early months of the contagion. Grey had vomited more than once. But the smell eventually became commonplace and bearable, to the point where he no longer noticed it. They were coming up to another settlement. Another village of the damned. The worst of times were over, people said. But it still didn't feel like the best of times would be ahead.

It was the middle of the day but still it was deathly quiet. The road, or rutted track cutting a scar through fallow fields, was empty, save for Gower and Grey. There would likely be rooms at various inns on the way to Windsor, those that were still open.

The great pestilence - or "God's chevauchee" as Grey had nicknamed it - had ravaged all. In the east, where the disease appeared to have originated from, they called it the "great year of annihilation." For once, the Muslims were being truthful, instead of being prone to exaggeration, in their rhetoric. "A just God now visits the sons of men and lashes the world," the king had remarked, his normally strong countenance drooping with pity. The supposed greatest minds of the age, at a medical faculty in Paris, explained the contagion as being caused by "an unusual conjunction of Saturn, Mars, and Jupiter." Some inexplicably, or perhaps predictably, blamed the Jews for the blight - and punished them accordingly. Grey had read a report that Basel had rounded up its Jews on an island in the Rhine and burned them. The Jews of Strasburg were forced into a cemetery, slaughtered and incinerated too. The pestilence addled one's wits, as well as one's body. King Magnus II of Sweden believed that his people should fast on a Friday and walk barefoot on a Sunday in order to assuage the wrath of the Almighty. Every week Grey would receive a letter from a friend pronouncing that it was the End of the World. Worse, some of his friends had started to writing poetry, which they asked him to read. Readings from Revelations eclipsed those from the Gospels during church services. Cures were tried (bloodletting, sweating, vomiting) and found wanting. Herbs - and poisons - were administered. Flagellants whipped themselves, to pay for the sins of Man. "They should whip themselves harder," was Grey's advice. Perhaps more than a third of the populace had perished, within just eighteen months or so. Few died peacefully.

Most died in agony. Grief hung over the realm like louring clouds, blocking out the light. Conversation consisted of sharing news about who had died. Crosses were kissed. Prayers offered up, disappearing into the ether like the fumes from funeral pyres. Grey had often remarked that life is a joke, with death as its punchline - but the comment no longer amused him. London, smoking like hell from various cremation pits, was even more unpleasant than usual, if that could be possible. Many noblemen retreated to their country estates, although the highest and strongest walls could be breached by the pestilence. The plague was Godlike. People proved they were all too mortal. The entire country was under siege, or being sacked, the spymaster fancied. Or every soul felt like they were due to take part in a forlorn hope. The clergy suffered more than most, as many elected to take care of the sick - and contracted the disease in the process. Grey encountered a local priest, barely able to walk, his figure misshapen with buboes the size of tennis balls. Perhaps in a bid to perish himself, Grey had visited a close friend on his deathbed. All the man wanted, at the end, was for someone to hold his hand. It was the last thing that members of his family wanted to do, however. As much as Grey did not fear his own passing, he did not want to abandon Eleanor. Life needed to go on, if it could. The king suffered - and not just because he grieved for his "dearest daughter". The spymaster and the monarch shared more than one letter. Grey had also visited Edward at Windsor. "I feel as useless as a eunuch in a brothel. Our body politic is sick, and its head cannot provide a cure. Faith and hope feel like they are ebbing away, like a tide that will not return… The damned contagion is a dragon I'm unable to smite. There is no one to assassinate, to blackmail or bribe to end this war. This series of losing battles. Its hunger is never satisfied," the king confessed, his head in his hands. Despair as legion as death. "All that I fixed after my father's reign is now coming undone. Unseeded and unharvested fields scar the landscape. Soldiers, who had once defended our shores, have turned into brigands. Justinian had his plague. Will they name this plague after me one day? I would prefer to make my mark in the history books in a different way… I suffer a recurring nightmare about waking up and seeing my wife and Edward afflicted with blotches and buboes. Being marked for death.

It all seems so real. It all could be so real... God help us all, if God is not the one punishing us." Despite the danger to himself the king still toured parts of the country, witnessing the suffering firsthand and visiting his subjects, like a general attempting to raise the morale of his troops. As well as cherishing the company of Eleanor, Sir Hugh was grateful for the man-at-arms being part of his household, if only to have someone to drink with each evening. Even the nobleman's wine cellar may not have been copious enough to drown their sorrows though. The two friends attempted to retain their good humour in the face of various horrors. "I can't even punch a Flagellant to make myself feel better," Gower half-joked. "The only reason not to do it would be that the bastard would probably enjoy it... At least this pestilence has proved that we are all equal in the eyes of God. Because we're all damned." Yet there were flickers of light in the darkness. Perhaps all was not lost. England remained England. Still a green and pleasant land, in places. In the same way that Grey and Gower's sense of humour held and there was wine left in the cellar, there was still enough common decency and Christian feeling throughout the country. Society didn't entirely collapse. It wasn't quite the End of the World.

Rain freckled the air and their faces as they rode on. The mizzle numbed Gower's stony face. If only it could numb his heart too. The man-at-arms worried about Eleanor. He felt he left part of himself behind. He could logically conclude that she would be safe where she was. But logic and love hold little commerce with one another. Before parting Eleanor had given Gower a small vial of her perfume. She also instructed the soldier to write her a letter for every week he was away. Grey would ensure that any correspondence reached her. It was a bittersweet feeling as he remembered saying goodbye earlier in the day.

"Are you going to miss me then?" Gower remarked.

"Yes, who else am I going to be able to beat at chess in the evening?"

"Anyone you play, I warrant."

She smiled, prettily. But there was longing and loss behind the young woman's comely features.

"And will you miss me?"

"Yes. I'll definitely miss your cooking," Gower joked, trying to lighten a mood which felt as leaden as the skies.

Eleanor laughed. The sound was like his favourite song. But then her bright eyes prickled with tears as she gazed at the soon to be departing soldier. He would have to survive both the pestilence and combat to return home safely. She buried her head in his chest to hide her grief and tears. She wanted to tell him she loved him - and that she did not want him to leave. But Eleanor knew she couldn't. Shouldn't. At the same time Gower wanted to put the words together to ask her to marry him. But the words escaped him, like sand falling through an hourglass. They held one another for a moment - or an eternity.

Gower and Grey finally set off, into the headlong bitter wind. The man-at-arms gave into temptation and stared back at Eleanor, who remained in sight until the woods swallowed him up. She wrapped her woollen shawl around her and bowed her head, her shoulders convulsing as she sobbed, as if she were a chrysalis which wouldn't turn into a butterfly until he returned.

A murder of crows suddenly left their perches of spindly branches on a brace of silver birch trees and swooped to the ground, hoping that worms would come to the surface in the rain.

Gower scrutinised the landscape and remembered that he had taken part in a tournament in the area several years ago. The fields had been a lush green. Ladies wore shimmering dresses in the clement sunshine. Pits were dug to roast wood pigeons and wild boar rather than inter the dead. The man-at-arms had taken part in fencing bouts, as opposed to jousts, and put many a knight on his arse. Knights who had recently become members of the prestigious Order of the Garter. He had bested the best. Gower smiled as he recalled the coin he earned that day from placing wagers on himself. He also pictured Sir Edmund Wingfield's flushed countenance when the nobleman lost to the lowly infantryman for the second time. Sir Edmund proceeded to insult Gower, accusing him of cheating. "He has no honour to impugn!" the knight protested. "You're impugning your own honour now, Edmund. Apologise, or you'll be impugning my honour as the host of this tournament," the king pronounced, his words as hard as iron. The nobleman duly asked the common soldier's forgiveness, his face red with shame rather than indignation.

"How do you intend to find Creton?" Gower asked, breaking the comfortable silence between the two friends.

"The plan will be to draw him out and have him find me," Sir Hugh Grey answered, as the sartorial spy straightened the fur-lined hat on his head. "My French counterpart has shot his bolt. I will not allow him to shoot again. There's scant honour among spies, as you may imagine. Better to eat the dog then let the dog eat you. My last intelligence report places him outside of Rennes. He has been serving his own interest in the name of the crown, again. The pestilence denuded him of some of his revenues and duties, but he has found others in their wake. Creton is a man possessed, as zealous as any pope, in terms of enriching himself. He has recently been blackmailing husbands, threatening to denounce wives as being witches. He appropriates the estates of noblemen who he outs as being enemies of the state. Creton is wise enough to share some of his spoils with the exchequer, so the authorities turn a blind eye to his crimes. There are those in Philip's court who wish to see him punished for his sins in this life rather than the next, though. I will need to put a few things in place before we make our crossing. Springes to catch woodcocks, to quote a phrase. We will first see the king at Windsor. Be prepared to endure a day or two of quarantine... Edward is in good health, I believe. The principal malady he may be suffering from is tedium, which is a symptom of the peace. The king is itching to commit to a campaign once more. As is the Prince of Wales. He is keen to make a name for himself. He needs to make money too, I imagine, to fund his expenditure. Like his father, the prince will not spend one pound when he can spend ten. He is a generous young man, but he is generous with the taxes of the others. A campaign would grant the prince an opportunity to capture spoils from the enemy. You have barely seen the prince since Crécy, I suspect."

"Yes," Gower replied. The soldier had fought side by side with the heir to the throne during the bloody battle and had saved his life. Despite their discrepancy in their rank, the prince considered the man-at-arms a friend. After Gower returned to England the prince had written him on more than one occasion, enclosing an expensive gift when he did so. The soldier possessed a pair of silk gloves that would have befitted Eleanor more, as well as a glass perfume bottle (which he kept spare nails in). Gower had been pleased when he heard how the prince had acquitted himself well at tournaments. He was also, understandably, a founder member of the Order of the Garter.

"The only conquests he can speak of lately are those made in the bedchamber," Grey added, in a spirit of amusement rather than admonishment. The smile faded from the spy's visage, however, as he rode past a lone gravestone by the side of the road. The sight was not now uncommon. Such burial plots had sprung up like wildflowers across the country. Grey slowed to read the inscription:

"For my dearest wife and child. You are in a better, fairer place now."

The satirical spy was tempted to issue the comment that most places were better and fairer than the current corner of Cornwall they were venturing through - but desisted. Despite having just adjusted his hat on his head, he removed the cap out of respect. Grey remembered his own family and sympathised with his fellow widower's sentiments.

3.

Raymon Creton knew that all was not well when his manservant, Rollant, announced that Guarin was at his door, as opposed to Arnaud Bernier. The captain had been brave and dutiful enough to send a couple of men ashore to locate Bernier and his other passengers. Guarin concluded that their mission had failed when the report came back that the Englishman was alive and had just departed with his household. The English man-at-arms had also been observed burning several bodies that morning in a corner on the grounds of the property.

The spymaster flirted with the idea of rewarding the captain for his enterprise and diligence, but then conveniently forgot. Creton spared little thought for Bernier and the men he had lost, save for cursing their failure. Whether Grey had interrogated Bernier or not, the Frenchman assumed that his counterpart would suspect him of being behind the assassination attempt. Creton expected that Grey would try to pay him in kind. But the Englishman would have to find him first.

Creton dismissed the captain and his manservant with an abrupt word and wave of his hand, leaving him to stew in the reception room of a property he appropriated just outside of Caen. Creton had purchased the chateau after the spy had denounced the previous owner as a traitor to the crown - and the exchequer had sold the asset to the high-ranking official at a substantial discount. The main house was by far the grandest in the area. Outbuildings were home to careworn servants and Creton's retinue of bodyguards.

The window looked out upon a bright, picturesque aspect of fields and pasture, glistening from a recent shower. Choice artworks, liberated from the estates of other enemies of France, furnished the walls. A custom-made cabinet dominated the far corner of the room, which contained a custom-made strongbox. The strongbox, which would be difficult to move and even more difficult to open, housed the spy's private papers, composed using a cypher that only a handful of people in the kingdom could decode. A fire roared from the hearth.

As much as the master of the house ensured that the rooms he used were warmed at all times, he policed the amount of firewood that the servants could burn through.

Creton slumped into a cushioned chair, wearing a garment which resembled a cassock. It was difficult to know whether his face was flush from the heat - or from the frustration and anger that Sir Hugh Grey was still drawing breath. He had half-hoped that the pestilence would have eliminated his enemy, but when the opportunity arose of purchasing the intelligence for where the Englishman was living - along with Auclair's daughter - the spymaster decided to act. Grey had evaded capture once before, on the eve of the Battle of Crécy. Rivals at court had mocked him for his failure, saying that "sometimes it's the bigger fish which slips through the net". The Englishman ran agents under his nose in Paris. Sir Hugh Grey was the pebble in his shoe which he couldn't remove. A weeping sore. Bernier deserved to die in the face of his failure. At no point would Creton countenance that he was somehow to blame for the botched mission.

During the past few years, the Frenchman had amassed a fortune. He was now wealthier than many of the noblemen at court who looked down their aquiline noses at the low-born official. Creton had put on considerable weight from living the good life. His once lean, flinty features were now jowly. His tailor had to alter a number of his clothes over the past year. His tonsured hair was now completely iron-grey. Cruel eyes glinted like polished coins in the firelight. Women seldom found him attractive, even when they realised how wealthy the official was. Not that Creton was particularly interested in having women desire him - or desiring them in return. "Women are weak, yet potent enough to prove a weakness," Evrard Fossat, Creton's predecessor and mentor, advised. "Spare yourself the vexation and expense involved in procuring a wife, Raymon. Marriage is not a reward, but a punishment. Instead of a wife, just arrange for a whore to live with you who can also cook and clean. She will doubtless cost you less." It was rumoured, however, that Fossat preferred catamites to courtesans.

The official's hands were stained with ink and metaphorical blood. The table next to him contained a piece of correspondence, which had occupied Creton's thoughts before Rollant's arrival. News had reached him of a plot to bribe one of the captains commanding a gate and take back Calais from the English. Creton's first response was to feel aggrieved and insulted, that he hadn't been consulted in relation to the mission. If he confronted the authors of the conspiracy, they would defend themselves by asserting that the fewer people knew about the mission, the greater the secrecy would be. The spymaster had employed the argument and excuse before, when keeping his enemies in the dark about his actions. As much as the plot contained an element of subterfuge, the mission would be led by Geoffrey de Charny, according to his informant. The feted knight was a capable commander, although Creton felt that his advancement had been a result of lineage rather than merit.

The king looked on de Charny favourably, being untainted by the defeat at Crécy, but Creton consoled himself with the scenario that Philip would soon look on him favourably, if his current plan came to fruition. The spy had received a coded message yesterday, through a trusted intermediary, from an agent based in the heart of the English court. Sir Robert Seton had informed Creton that he was in possession of a packet of compromising letters, penned by the English king. Intimate love letters, addressed to various conquests and mistresses. Seton had proved a reliable source of intelligence in the past. Although he was close to the king - Edward often asked Seton to participate in tournaments and join him on hunting excursions around Windsor - the nobleman had not been invited into the Order of the Garter. The slighted nobleman had repaid perceived disloyalty with treachery. Seton was now a prized asset, providing ongoing intelligence in relation to the king's activities and intentions. The indulged aristocrat was proposing a high fee for his treasure trove of compromising material, but the price would be worth paying, Creton believed. At the very least the letters would humiliate Edward. His infidelities and sins, laid bare to the world, would also undermine the king in the eyes of the clergy and his parliament. Seton stipulated in his message that he wanted to receive the money and hand over the letters in person, at a mutually agreed location. Given the significant sum involved, Seton also posited that their exchange would be their final piece of business together. Creton would agree to the Englishman's terms, but the Frenchman would not hesitate in breaking his promise if circumstances demanded. It would of course be easy to blackmail the knight after he betrayed the king, as the Frenchman could threaten to expose the nobleman as the source of the letters. Perhaps he could also extract the whereabouts of Sir Hugh Grey from the Englishman when they finally met. Seton might even be willing to set a trap for Grey or poison him.

Raymon Creton permitted himself a thin, cruel smile as he thought of disgracing the English king, seeing the enemy expelled from Calais and eliminating his counterpart. All would be well.

CALAIS

4.

Despite, or because of the cold, Edward of Woodstock - the Prince of Wales - kept to his regime of undertaking fencing practise at midday. A chill wind cut through him more than any blade could, he felt. The visor was down on his pig-snouted helmet. Should he have raised it one would have seen a young man with a strong jaw, intelligent eyes and pleasant features. Although his features would soon become less pleasant, when engaged in combat.

A dull light illuminated the courtyard in Windsor castle which housed the patch of grass where the practise bout would take place.

The much-lauded prince was mindful of ignoring the two doe-eyed young women, draped in furs, who sat on a bench at the end of the courtyard. They were Margaret and Katherine. Sisters. Daughters of Sir Ralph Wigmore. The prince briefly wondered if Sir Ralph knew that his daughters were now slightly less virtuous than they had been a month ago. He also wondered if the sisters knew that the prince had bedded them both. Like men, women were not incapable of deceiving one and all. The more time he had spent in the company of the fairer sex, the less fair they became, he fancied. Yet still he enjoyed the chase. He heard them giggle on more than one occasion, perhaps to try to entice him to look their way. Their eyes sparkled like the semi-precious gems they wore. The prince was perhaps amused rather than enamoured by their behaviour. He still hadn't decided which sister he would invite to his bedchamber that evening. He grinned in the privacy of his helmet as he imagined how he might one day invite both maidens to share his bed - at the same time. The virile nobleman soon shook such morish thoughts from his head, however. He needed to focus on the task at hand. Thomas Damory was an accomplished opponent. He shouldn't be underestimated. Damory had competed, with distinction, at various tournaments throughout Europe. The knight had also acquitted himself well on campaign, fighting bravely - and brutally - at Caen and Crécy. To keep his opponent honest and motivated, the prince had offered Damory a pair of ornate gauntlets, crafted from Spanish steel, should he be able to put him on the ground and make him yield.

A few more figures appeared in the courtyard to swell the number of shivering spectators. A smattering of courtiers no doubt were standing ready to applaud the increasingly influential heir to the throne.

The prince pulled on the straps of his shield and, despite the stiffness from the cold, drew his blunted broadsword from its scabbard. Damory, his features as frozen as the water pipes, lowered his visor and nodded, indicating that he was ready.

The tall knight launched himself forward, with a roar. Despite the weight of his armour his feet came off the ground. The prince quickly lifted his shield, almost above his head, to deflect the attack. His whole body juddered but the prince planted his boots in the soft turf and stood his ground.

The competitors proceeded to trade heavy blows, as swords pounded upon shields like hammers pounding away on anvils. Occasionally, the blunted blades would scrape against one another, causing the teeth of spectators to itch. The combatants were well-matched, although one felt that the prince was fighting within himself or weighting his strategy towards defence rather than attack. Every now and then a lunge or swing would get past the shield or sword, but the glancing hit was never significant enough to force their opponent off balance. Damory's breathing became laboured. The knight was perhaps not in peak condition, with the pestilence preventing the hosting of any tournaments across the country. Yet he fought on. The prince was also experienced enough to know how some noble knights would pretend to be tired, to lure their opponent into a false sense of confidence. But Edward of Woodstock had formulated his own plan. Up until now he had only used his shield as a defensive instrument. But training with Gower years ago had taught the young prince how to utilise any buckler as an offensive weapon too.

When the combatants came together once more, sweat dripping down their contorted faces beneath their visors, the prince brought his sword back, as if motioning to strike. Damory moved in turn to block any prospective hit. But the prince, instead of bringing his blade forward, punched his shield into the side of the knight's bascinet. Several onlookers winced at the clanging sound of the blow. Damory was disorientated, long enough to become further disorientated after the prince unleashed another, more powerful blow which knocked the knight to the ground. Edward of Woodstock lost little time in standing over the defeated competitor. The rounded tip of his blade hung over Damory's throat, forcing him to yield. He could hear both ringing and sycophantic applause in his ears.

The prince sheathed his sword and held out a hand to help his opponent to his feet. The heir to the throne offered up some kind words to the soldier. Later that evening he would still present the Spanish gauntlets to his new friend, as a token of his gratitude.

Although his son could not see him on the balcony, which perched over the courtyard, Edward of Windsor still offered up a nod of approval and appreciation. Dressed in just an embroidered jacket and cloak, the king had no desire to show weakness and shiver. It had been a fine display. Thomas Damory was no pup or peacock, but a seasoned warrior. Edward couldn't help but think upon whether his son could best him, as easily as he bested Damory. His sword arm might now be stronger, swifter, than his father's. During his formative years Edward had hired all manner of fencing and jousting tutors to school his son and make a warrior out of him. But he presently had little left to learn. The prince now trained himself - work-hardening his body like a piece of iron. He had proved himself on the battlefield and in tournaments, in jousts and melees. He had been included in the Order of the Garter through merit rather than patronage, his father proudly judged. The cub was now a lion.

Edward retreated into his musty study and sat down, his chin buried in his chest. Weary. Was it the cold or his age making his joints stiff? His body seemed to be rusting, like a once fine suit of armour past its prime. Maps and correspondence littered the table. He couldn't be bothered to stoke the fire - or to even order a servant to do so - and tend to his administrative duties. He had grown tired of holding a pen. He wished to wield his sword again. But a flicker of a smile animated his features. Perhaps he might soon draw his weapon once more. The king drained the wine from his cup. If the vintage was once sweet, it now tasted sour.

I am older. But am I any wiser? Or closer to achieving my

ambition? My fate? One either moves forwards or backwards in life. One advances or retreats…

The burden of the English crown was a heavy one. But somehow that burden would only lighten when he wore the French crown too, Edward believed.

He recalled the moment at Antwerp, when he had announced his claim to the French throne. War was inevitable. But the king and the country were ready for war. He had subsequently won great victories at Sluys and Crécy. He had won prestige and collected booty - but unfortunately not enough to win him financial freedom from Florentine bankers. He also still needed to go cap in hand to parliament each year to raise taxes for his campaigns. For all the money spent, the arrows unleashed, the blood spilled, Edward seemed no closer to securing the crown to when he had stood in Antwerp. What had he actually won?

Calais. After the victory at Crécy the English army remained unopposed. Edward marched north to capture the valuable trading port. Such prized assets are well protected though. The town was fortified with walls, moats, ditches and towers. Jean de Vienne, the commander of Calais, could afford to be defiant. Plans were discussed, to storm the fortifications with siege engines or mine the walls. But the only genuine option was to starve the town into surrendering. It would be a war of attrition, on both sides. Roads and sea lanes were blocked off to prevent the inhabitants being re-supplied. But Edward struggled to re-supply his army, with men and victuals, too. England and France were emptied of surplus provisions. Edward's army camp grew into a veritable town in itself, with make-shift markets, taverns and other amenities - including a brothel or two for bored and lusty soldiers. Judging that the English king was distracted, King David of Scotland invaded the auld enemy and laid waste to vulnerable settlements just below the border, believing that only "wretched monks, lewd priests, swineherds, cobblers and skinners" remained to defend England. He was wrong, to his cost. The Scottish monarch was distracted by dreams of glory and overextended himself. Spearmen, archers and capable commanders marched north to defeat the Scots at the Battle of Neville's Cross. King David, his body playing host to a couple of arrowheads to remind him of his folly, was captured and imprisoned in the Tower of London. But still Calais proved a bastion of defiance.

Summer turned to winter - and winter brought disease and death. The only seeds being sown were those of doubt. Morale dropped, as low as the temperature. The bloody flux ate away at the stagnating army, cutting down more men than any French blades had done. Soldiers, who had withstood wave after wave of French cavalry at Crécy, could be seen groaning and writhing in agony on the ground, clutching their bellies. Vomiting blood. Edward felt the strain, like a creaking bow about to break. Jean de Vienne was feeling the strain too and, to preserve dwindling food supplies, expelled the women, children and infirm from the town, abandoning them to the no-man's land between the two forces. Initially Edward would not allow the civilians to travel through the siege lines. Some perished, until the king relented and granted them passage. No amount of wine could wash away the rage and frustration he felt at the time. Soldiers became bored as well as ill and took to quarrelling and looting. Some longbowmen and spearmen even deserted. Horses died - and Edward couldn't help but note how some noblemen mourned their mounts more than their men.

Winter turned to spring. The siege continued, like a seemingly endless funeral service. The stranglehold around the town grew tighter, as reports came through of inhabitants eating cats and dogs - and even rats. The English were at least winning logistical victories, as foodstuffs and men were re-supplied. In order to preserve what was left of the town's rations, de Vienne decided to eject several hundred additional mouths that he was unable to feed. This time Edward refused safe passage for the civilians - and not just because it was rumoured that the townsfolk may have contained spies, intending to deliver intelligence to the French king. "The bastards need to be punished, not pardoned," William de Bohun, the Earl of Northampton, argued. The refugees were left to die, being denied food and water. Philip of France eventually raised an army to challenge the besiegers and dispel the enemy - but Edward mustered his own forces and sent the French into a customary retreat.

Calais surrendered - and was duly sacked. Riches were plundered and the French expelled. The port would serve as an English colony. The town was a bridgehead into the rest of France. Calais was

English soil, and Edward would defend it as such.

The king's features tightened as he lifted his head and glared at the map, displaying England and France, on the wall. The two kingdoms. His two kingdoms. The gap of the Channel between the two was but a couple of inches on the chart. Close, but also a world away.

Calais was dearly bought - perhaps too dearly bought - which was why Edward would not countenance for it to be relinquished or sold cheaply. The king had received intelligence the day before that a French force, commanded by Geoffrey de Charny, was intending to take back the town. A bribe had been offered to Amerigo de Pavia, a captain of Calais, to open the gates to the French. Edward received intelligence concerning the betrayal. Arrangements were being put in place to strengthen the garrison, in defence of any attack. But Edward was beginning to seed another idea. He wanted to give the enemy a bloody nose, so the French curs thought twice about sniffing around his property again. The king instructed Amerigo to pretend to accept the bribe of forty thousand florins. Geoffrey de Charny would prove a worthy opponent. History would record the encounter. It was also time to deploy the Order of the Garter. The country needed to feel some purpose and pride again. The king needed to feel some purpose and pride again. It was a moment to carry bloodied swords, not just ceremonial blades, once more. "I fear I might die of boredom, rather than the pestilence, if I am cooped up here any longer," Edward had confessed to Sir Robert Seton a couple of days ago.

The king's chin was no longer buried in his chest. A mane of hair framed an imperious countenance once more. His heart began to gallop rather than trot. Edward was resolved to cross the Channel himself and defend Calais. Lead the Order of the Garter, his new round table of knights. His beloved wife would make a face when telling her that he would be leaving for another campaign. Her expression would grow even more disapproving upon hearing the news that her eldest son would be joining the king of his latest great and glorious adventure. But the queen was always making faces. The king would not be made to feel guilty for doing his duty to his kingdom. Edward did feel twinges of guilt sometimes, though, when he caught his wife staring at him, as he in turn desirously glared at the young women at court (often the wives or daughters of noblemen) who he intended to take as mistresses.

5.

Others shivered and retched, disposing of the contents of their stomachs over the sides of the rolling ship. The foaming sea belched and churned - as if it might swallow or spit out the vessel ploughing its way across the Channel. Edward remained as watchful and stoic as the wooden hawk carved upon the prow of the ship. If he felt seasick, he refused to show it. His son, standing next to the king, did his best to imitate his father. But occasionally his legs would wobble, or his face grow pale, or another colour, in anticipation of vomiting.

The voices of soldiers - a few singing and laughing but most emitting more bestial sounds - could be heard in the background, along with the whinnying of anxious horses stabled in the hold of the vessel. The wind slapped into the sails, like a rebuke. An adviser courteously and cautiously mentioned to his king that it might be prudent for the sovereign and his heir to sail in different boats, citing the tragedy of the White Ship (when William Adelin, the only son of Henry I, had perished during the sinking of the vessel), which in turn plunged England into a succession crises and the Anarchy.

"We should not tempt fate," Sir Gilbert Russell argued, who was paid to worry and often worked overtime.

"We will be fine. I thank the stars that I'm not superstitious," Edward replied, with a wry smile.

The shoreline of England melted into the soupy, grey mist behind them. Grey clouds and a greyer sea, through a needling mizzle, lay ahead. The landscape seemed like a giant piece of slate to the prince, waiting for someone to scrawl upon it. He wondered what might happen should he encounter de Charny himself during any engagement. The prince had heard stories about his victories in tournaments. He had once unseated an opponent during a joust with only half a lance. He asked his father if he intended to seek out de Charny on the battlefield - and what would happen to him if he captured the Frenchman?

"I have no desire to kill so fine a gentleman, but I am determined to best him and his forces. I will protect my people and property.

Bribing one's way into a stronghold may not be the most honourable course of action, but de Charny is not without honour. We will treat him according to his rank and character."

"I apologise for the rough crossing, sire," the captain of the Alfred remarked, wringing his hands and bowing to his king. George Crabbe was balding and walked with a stoop. He had a tired or mournful face, or both, having lost his wife to the pestilence earlier in the year. The widower was struggling to bring up his three children - and struggling to find a new wife who could take over his parental duties.

"I do not hold you accountable for the weather, George. I am the king - and even I have scant influence in regard to how the elements behave. Cnut could not hold back the tide - and not even King Arthur or Merlin could snap their fingers and bid the rain to stop. But I do have it in my power to reward you and your crew for giving us passage in such inclement weather," Edward declared with a smile, albeit the captain was unsure how to react. He decided not to tell the crew about their prospective bonus, lest it prove underwhelming or unpaid. Kings can be as capricious as the weather.

"I know that I have told you this before, drunk and sober, but a king has two principal duties," Edward pensively remarked, after the captain departed to tend to his ship. Crabbe's voice would soon grow hoarse in the background from having to bark out orders above the clamour of the rough crossing. "Permit me to bore you again. A king must first provide security for his subjects and uphold justice at home. I have been unable to keep my people safe from the great mortality, however. I sometimes feel like I wear the mark of Cain. I tried to ignore the disease at first, hoping that it would just blow away like an ill wind. But ignorance isn't bliss, my son. I then did my best to combat the pestilence. But my best was far from good enough. The enemy could not be fought in the lists. Not even St George can slay a dragon which he cannot see. I have been told that God sent the disease to punish sinners. It seems that there are plenty of sinners out there, even more than one can imagine perhaps. The first sin is the denial of sin. I do not deny my sins, they may be as numerous as the spots of rain surrounding us, but your sister did not deserve to be punished for her sins, if she possessed any," the king asserted, his usually commanding voice breaking a little, like cracks appearing in panes of glass, as he pictured his teenaged daughter Joan, who had perished from the pestilence on the eve of her marriage. Her tragic passing had seared itself into his soul. "The sting of grief cuts deeper that any wound on the battlefield," Edward had confided to his old friend, William de Bohun. The prince found it difficult to discern whether raindrops or tears were meandering down his father's cheeks. The strain on his countenance was clear, though only he could see it as his father faced forward still at the bow. The merciless disease may have spared the king thus far, but it had aged him. "The second duty as a sovereign is to prosecute one's enemies abroad. I cannot tilt my lance at this unholy - or God sent - pestilence, but I can ride out against the damned French. Perhaps I am trying to overcompensate. But I must do something, for fear of withering on the vine. My task is to pass on a kingdom greater to that from what I received. I owe you and my subjects that much."

"You do not have to carry any burden by yourself, father. Your enemies are my enemies. I will serve as your spear tip once more, as I did at the vanguard at Crécy, if called upon. If you have affairs to tend to at home, then let me lead your campaigns abroad."

The king nodded his head, either in agreement with the idea or approving of his son's support.

Owain of Swansea felt sick. Not because of the dreaded plague, or the nausea caused by the uneasy pitch of the listing vessel, but the Welsh archer cursed his fate from losing at dice - again. The soldier didn't even much feel like drinking to wash away his sorrows, albeit he habitually finished his ale. Such had been his run of bad luck against his fellow longbowmen, Richard Maldon, the vintenar who he served under, had advanced him over half of his pay. And it was now gone. The money had passed through his hands quicker than if he had spent a night in a brothel.

He swore in Welsh and English as he abandoned the table, bumping his head upon the beam above him as he did so. The bowman consoled himself with the fact that he was travelling across the Channel with his old friend. There were few men, if any, who the archer would rather fight - or drink - with. Gower was a good man, despite being English, the Welshman had joked to his companion earlier in the week. They had spent an evening together catching up over a pitcher of ale - as well as a jug of mulled wine and jug of mead. Owain only had a vague recollection of what his friend told him. He was pleased to hear how Gower had bagged the fine French lass who they had rescued, the night before the Battle of Crécy.

"You did save her life, Will. It's the least she can do, to let you tup her each night or cook a meal for you. If she does both then you really are a lucky bastard. I'd say you're all but married, but you seem too content to be husband and wife. You're certainly luckier than me, given my run at the dice table recently… Aye, that Eleanor was a fine woman, if I remember rightly. Far finer than you, of course. She was smart, handsome and well-mannered. But they say that opposites attract… I missed you during the siege at Calais. God, that was a hard slog. I thought, like a Welsh ballad, that it would never end. It wasn't just a season in hell, it was several seasons. Even I got bored with the taverns and trollops in the camp. We lost some good men capturing that bastard town. The bitch wouldn't open her legs and let us have our wicked way with her. But our king is as bloody minded as a Welsh woman - and we took the port. I got my share of some loot and I headed home, thinking that I'd be off campaigning again within the year. But then the pestilence came. The seasons in hell of Calais felt like heaven compared to those times. It felt like the end of days. Death was all powerful. More powerful than God. I would rather now see a hundred French soldiers charging towards me than just one poor soul benighted with the boil… Richard let me stay on a corner of his land. I kept myself to myself. It was as cold as a harridan's scowl during winter, but freezing to death felt better than other fates. I was able to grow some food and he let me hunt in his woods. There are foxes which haven't eaten as many rabbits as I have over the past year. Richard tried his best to keep his family safe, but he lost a couple of bairns to the damned disease. They were sweet children. Don't talk to me about the justice of the Almighty and original sin. It's just a bastard disease in a bastard world. Folk were going to bed feeling fine and waking up dead. Not even the English have cursed the Welsh as much as the pestilence… But I'll depress myself and turn to drink if I'm not careful. It's good to see you Will, so it is. I'm glad God, or the Devil, spared you. Just make sure that the old spy doesn't get you killed on some fool's errand. He schemes more than a woman, that one. War is good for bringing old friends together, at least. I'm not sure what else it's good for. Aside drinking, whoring and earning some coin, of course. And to give kings something to do."

CALAIS

Owain swayed from side to side, due to drink or his lack of sea legs, as he made his way through the bowels of the ship and found his friend, tending to and calming his horse - a small but powerful black mare named Diana. The man-at-arms knew that if he looked after his mount then the creature would look after him in return, whether riding towards or away from the fighting.

Diana crunched upon an apple, swishing her glossy tail, visibly enjoying the treat.

"That horse eats better than I do," the Welshman said, extracting some pottage from in between his less than gleaming teeth, with his less than gleaming fingernail.

"I wouldn't be too envious. The apple is as sour as one of your moods, after losing at a game of dice."

"It's not the losing I mind so much, but it's losing to the English which smarts. I only seem to be able to beat the Irish these days, which isn't the greatest boast I'll grant you. They're as dim as a cloudy night sky, as thick as the walls at Calais. You can see why my mood should be so bloody sour."

"And what's the mood of Richard and the rest of the company?" Gower asked, as he commenced to use a grooming brush on his mount.

"Some are better for taking money off a Welshman, I imagine. It's good that Richard is about to be climb into the saddle once again. He could use the distraction. There were too many ghosts haunting him back home. Soldiers need to fight. What else are we good for?"

"It's been a while since the company has been on campaign. They may be out of practise."

"I can't speak for others, but if I can put an arrow into a scurrying rabbit then I'm sure I can stick a few into a fat, French knight astride a sway-backed palfrey."

The Welshman may have wondered if the peace and pestilence had made his friend soft, but Gower had told the archer about the French raid and attack on the cottage. The man-at-arms was ready to fight, as a priest is ever ready to pray.

6.

The king finished his lunch. The table may have been square rather than round, but he gathered his knights around it, both members of the Order of the Garter (including Sir John Beauchamp, Lord Mortimer and Lord Stafford) as well as others (Lord Manny, Sir John Montagu and Lord Berkeley). As they ate their salted pork, washed down with wine and ale from the sovereign's own stores, the king briefed his men again on the mission at hand and encouraged questions and suggestions.

There had been one figure conspicuous by his absence around the table, but Edward now decided to call upon his spymaster, who was working away in a cabin that the king had provided for him.

He entered, without knocking - being the only man on the ship brave or important enough to do so. The tall king - he may have gained the nickname of "Longshanks" if it hadn't been taken by his forebear - bowed his head to avoid the low ceiling. The wind outside howled, as if baying for blood. Edward was perhaps baying too much for French blood to notice.

Sir Hugh Grey was sat in the corner of the cabin, a half-eaten plate of food on the table, accompanied by a half-empty cup of Claret. A book was propped up on the make-shift desk, covering a crucifix attached to the wall. Incense burned on a shelf above the table, expunging the piquant odour of horseshit afflicting most of the rest of the vessel. Grey appeared scrivener-focused, wheels upon wheels turning in the Oxford educated spy's mind. Even though the king was suddenly present his hand still danced across parchment as Grey composed another letter in his spidery handwriting, to be added to the various other documents littered around the chamber. Edward briefly smiled to himself, musing how his agent could have been writing to order a new pair of boots or giving instruction to an assassin to murder a cardinal. One never knew with Grey, or one didn't want to know. "The dark arts should remain in the shadows," the spy once remarked, with a glint in his eye.

Grey finished off the sentence and turned to take in his king and friend. The pestilence had aged him - but it had aged everyone. Crow's feet perched on his eyes. Worry lines were cut, like scars, into his forehead. It was a face which had seen a lot, Grey thought, but one which wanted to see more. Do more. As much as the king still cut a fine figure, was he past his prime? The prince now turned more heads and cut a finer figure, one could argue. Grey wondered how the king might feel about such a shift. Was he now fighting time, as well as a whole host of other enemies?

The man who would be King Arthur had already lived a full life, encountering triumph and tragedy in equal measure. And he could still live to be twice his current years. Edward had been every inch a king, ever since that night at Nottingham Castle when he had bravely stridden into the chamber to arrest Roger Mortimer, his mother's lover, to secure the crown. His crown. Edward had healed the wounds of his father's - and Mortimer's - rule. Mortimer's son had even become a great ally and served in the Order of the Garter. England had felt proud and prosperous again, before the plague, under Edward's reign. But as much as Edward knew how to forge friendships, he had a talent for making enemies too. Mars may have been less bellicose, Grey thought. Was this mission to Calais not a prelude to prosecuting the war in earnest again? Edward was not immune to making rash or poor decisions. But he was also not immune from being converted from making the wrong decision, whether by advisers or his wife. There were a lot worse women he could have married. Unfortunately, there were few who could have proved worse in relation to the mistresses he took to his bed. Grey realised that his father had provided him with his greatest lesson. Edward II had taught Edward III how a king shouldn't act. How to have friends rather than favourites, how to lead from the front rather than cower at the rear. How to offer his subjects a vision, rather than settle for defeat or decline.

"I've seen lawyers buried in less parchment," Edward remarked.

"Lawyers often get paid by the line, which would explain their inclination to write a lot," Sir Hugh Grey replied, adjusting the silk cap on his head so it wasn't quite positioned at such a jaunty angle.

"I have just briefed the Order again. They are ready. Their swords have not grown so rusty that they do not know how to draw them.

We are still in need of a plan. Have you gone through the correspondence from Amerigo?" the king enquired, as he took a seat on a chest by the door. Either his bones or the timbers of the ship creaked a little.

"More than once. I'm also familiar with the town and its environs. I've the seed of an idea that's taking root. I can furnish you with a plan, but not my presence. I must ask you to give me leave to execute my own assignment. I have some business in the region, which touches upon both a personal and professional matter.

"Should I ask what you are up to?"

"Ask me no questions and I will tell you no lies," the spy responded. "Let us just say that I'm intending to go on a hunting expedition. I appreciate that you can scarce afford to spare any men, but I need to borrow a company, or half a company, of archers. I wouldn't ask unless I needed to."

Edward paused, pursing his lips. His spymaster's loyalty - both from a sense of honour and justified animus towards the French - was unassailable. Grey had been by his side at Antwerp, having partly composed the king's historic speech. He had been one of the only people in the sovereign's inner circle to support Edward's decision to attack at the battle of Sluys. Grey had helped secure several loans with Florentine bankers to finance his war against France. The spy had killed for king and country - and worked tirelessly to develop an intelligence network. Grey had recruited agents at the heart of the French court. Grey had also cultivated relationships with the best wine merchants and tailors in England and on the continent - and shared his contacts with the king. Edward considered the nobleman a friend. He was good company, being able to hold his drink and a conversation - which partly explained why he had extracted so many secrets and forged so many relationships over the years. Edward was at pains to recall when Grey had asked for anything in return for his devoted service.

"You shall have what you need, my friend. Are you aiming to capture or kill your prey?"

"Both," Grey replied, devoid of emotion, as he poured his companion a cup of wine and gave a nod of gratitude.

"It seems that we are both at war again. As one horseman of the apocalypse, Disease, commences to retreat, another, War, charges forward once again. Death remains ever untethered and I fear Famine may frolic across the country soon, given the lack of labourers left in the land," Edward said, or sighed, with the lines along his brow seemingly growing deeper. "Man is born to trouble, as the sparks fly upwards - but the sparks now resemble a conflagration, I warrant, such has been the trouble we have seen of late. Not even Merlin could magic our strife away. Heavy is the head that wears the crown."

The two men briefly broke off their conversation as they heard slurred, guttural voices from outside the cabin.

"I feel like I'm going to retch up what I had last month, let alone what I've just eaten," a soldier exclaimed, stumbling to get on deck.

"God, or Neptune, help us," his companion enjoined, groaning. "I'm only getting on a boat once more again. And that's to come home. I've known women to be calmer than this this wind."

Grey permitted himself a brief smile, as did the king.

"They may fight like the devil, but they can also complain like hell. Heavy is the head that may wear the crown, as you say. So, is it still your ambition to wear another and resume the campaign against the French?"

"Yes, but as much as I may wish to bestride the world like a colossus this king is but a man. I need to tend to England. Some of the fights ahead will not require me wielding a sword. We need good governance. We are already suffering labour shortages. Crops need to be sown and harvested. Wages are already rising. The nobility are petitioning me to restrict the movement of peasants and limit their pay, else the economy will fall into ruin, and we will not be able to feed ourselves."

"They are landowners, they would say that. But you are right in that England will need its king in the years ahead."

"Part of my reasoning in committing to this excursion is to test my son and the Order. Edward can don his black armour and take the fight to the French in my stead. Do you believe he will be equal to the task?" the king and father asked, nervously biting his bottom lip. Concerned.

Sir Hugh Grey narrowed his eyes in thought, weighing up a hundred different factors in a few seconds. He then nodded, assuredly.

"I do. The prince is a credit to yourself and the realm."

"I'm just afraid for me, when it comes to the time to tell his mother. She will be far from pleased, to put it mildly. I've yet to face anyone in the list who scares me more," Edward joked.

Grey smiled, politely and vaguely, as he ruefully recalled his own wife, Grace. He struggled to remember a cross word between them. His father had warned him that he was courting someone far beneath him in rank, but there was no one he esteemed more. Grey had been one of the most fortunate men in the world when married to Grace - only to become one of the most unfortunate after her passing. He had never once thought of re-marrying or even courting again. A month or so after the funeral he would still wake in the middle of the night and place the palm of his hand next to the space on the bed where Grace slept, half dreaming that she might still be there. The palm of his hand would then ball itself into an angry fist. Grey kept a lock of his spouse's hair in a copy of her favourite book of poetry. The widower also saved a vial of his wife's perfume, which he would smell just to remind himself of her every once in a while. He had done so a month ago and broke down in tears. Fond tears. Bitter tears. When Eleanor heard him, she looked in upon her "uncle," as she called him.

"Are you feeling yourself?" the young woman asked, unused to seeing the Englishman so vulnerable and emotional.

"Yes, I'm afraid I am," he replied, half-jokingly, wiping the tears away from his eyes with the sleeves of his embroidered jacket.

After his wife and daughter were murdered, Grey felt like he was akin to some of the figures from classical mythology who he had read about during his studies at Oxford. Grief ate away at him - but didn't kill him. Like the punishment of Prometheus. Life was a constant struggle and disappointment, akin to the labour of Sisyphus. Work helped him get through the day. Drink helped. Eleanor helped. Killing Frenchmen helped. The spymaster still hoped that he would one day uncover the name of his enemy who had led the coastal raid, which resulted in the murder of his family. Grey sometimes thought how he had endured the trauma of the pestilence better than most because the world had already broken his back on its rack.

7.

Calais.

Only a select few in the town were made aware of the king's presence. The plan to thwart de Charny's forces relied on surprise and subterfuge. Edward had flirted with the idea of bringing along a poet or chronicler to accompany their party and record events, albeit the king seldom enjoyed sharing the same room as authors. They often used ten words when two would do - and they rivalled monarchs in their capacity for self-importance and self-love. Poets were also notorious for avoiding buying a drink, for themselves or others - believing they should have their libations bought for them.

"Are you going to feel comfortable, my liege, playing the part of a merchant?" Sir Hugh Grey asked, when briefing his sovereign, as they spied the walls of the port through the mist and clusters of seabirds.

"I've played the part of a king for nearly two score years. I'm sure I can play the role of a mere mortal. It'll be novel and refreshing, I warrant. It may prove a pleasure and relief, to be ignored," he remarked, although at the same time the king thought he might be offended too in not being recognised, given the number of images he had circulated amongst his people over the years. "As a commoner I will be able to fucking swear even more, although I'm not sure how much I will relish drinking the swill they serve up in the taverns. I will also only need to endure my humble station as a humble subject for a few days. I'm not sure if I could live a lie for much more than that, my friend," Edward replied, smiling broadly to himself.

"You will be fine. Every man deludes himself and lives a lie at some point. It may be the quality that makes him most a man," the spymaster replied, his voice the sound of a shrug.

It was strange seeing the walls of Calais again. The king felt a sense of pride at his achievement to capture the town. But he also experienced a sense of resentment. How many days had those walls and the stronghold's inhabitants defied him? How many English dead had they buried? Calais had been a thorn in his side, a tic buried so deep that Edward scarce believed, on some dark nights, that he would ever remove it. For so long he had wanted to pummel and punish the town. Now he would do almost anything to preserve his colony. After its capture there were those who rejoiced that the town had been "God-given." But Edward knew that Calais had been bought with blood, not prayers. Yet it was now a gem, hammered into the coastline. Another gem - an English gem - in what would form the crown of France.

Although bitterly cold, the dockers and others were out in force when Edward disembarked. Folk may have nursed a headache or two from their Christmas festivities, but the town was a hive of activity. It was whispered quietly, but the pestilence was retreating - and normality was returning. Trade, commerce and industry were recovering, like daffodils heralding spring. Smoke spiralled upwards from bakeries, as opposed to cremation pits. Bells were ringing out for weddings and baptisms, rather than from just mourning the dead. People were making a living - and paying their taxes. Men thankfully worried more about the pox than plague again. Even the Flagellants had moved on, seeking to find redemption elsewhere. Or, as some cynics claimed, many were just seeking attention. The streets were no longer filled with their caterwauling and the cringeworthy noise of their whips slapping into their scarred and scarlet backs. The winter weather had also perhaps cooled their ardour for saving the world and caused them to disband.

Edward couldn't help but laugh heartily - and he was even tempted to reward the man with a coin - when a carter cursed the king for walking out on the street and nearly being knocked down.

"Oi! Who do you think you are, thinking you've got right of way - bloody royalty?"

The king enjoyed the company of his salty subjects. He was not averse to buying rounds of drinks - and having drinks bought for him in return by strangers he befriended. He shook more than one hand and felt a sense of fraternity, rather than obsequiousness. The monarch didn't particularly miss being bowed to, though he would not prohibit the custom when he returned to his normal role.

Owain also experienced mixed emotions returning to the town

which he had besieged for so long. He remembered the sallow, dejected countenances of the French as they were evicted from their homes. It resembled a funeral procession. The image was soon replaced by the memory of thousands of sanguine, triumphant faces as the English entered Calais. Looting to their heart's content. The Welshman couldn't recall much about the following few days, just that he had a good time. The town was smashed open like a strongbox. The whores put up their prices, but the soldiers were too jubilant to complain.

The archer couldn't help but notice the similarities, as well as the differences, between the two warring sides. There was much to commend the English to the French, and vice-versa, if they could pause and stop slaughtering one another.

Icicles hung from roofs. Frost dusted chimneys. Although the weather was far from hospitable, there was much about the town that was welcoming and attractive, Gower mused. He fancied how Eleanor would enjoy visiting the port. There was a bookbinder and several dress shops. The streets echoed with laughter. Grey had mentioned how the French had not entirely been enamoured with King Philip and his rule. "They were taxed even more than they are under Edward, if you can believe it."

Gower would recommend to Eleanor that they visit the town together when the opportunity arose. Although would they do so as the man-at-arms serving as the lady's bodyguard, or as husband and wife? The question of whether the soldier should propose loomed large in his mind, far more than the impending engagement against the French.

Sir Hugh Grey, through employing a couple of his agents who were posted in Calais, arranged for the king and his party to lodge at an array of inns and properties throughout the town, so as not to bring attention to the fact that a small army had disembarked. Their horses were also stabled in various locations. Only a handful of people, including the garrison commander, were aware of the mission at hand.

The king approved of the spymaster's plan, so much so that Edward would claim it as his own.

"We have been through much together. We will get through this too. The offer still stands for you to join the ranks of the Order of the Garter one day, should you desire," Edward remarked, as Sir Hugh Grey escorted his king to his lodgings.

It was not the first time that the nobleman had received an invitation to join the prestigious and holy order. Sir Hugh had politely declined, arguing that the place should be awarded to someone more suitable. In his own mind, however, Grey thought himself either too honourable, or not honourable enough, to serve alongside his fellow knights.

The nobleman smiled and nodded in response to his sovereign's words, but he felt like after he had dealt with Creton his war would be over. Retirement, or at the very least semi-retirement, beckoned. He had once hoped to translate the epigrams of Martial into both French and English. But securing Eleanor's safety was all that mattered at present, even more than preserving his own existence. His life was only half a life, at best, without Grace. The king could afford to look to the future and dream of winning the French crown. But Sir Hugh dreamed of the past. He dreamed of his wife and child. He dreamed of seeing them again. He dreamed of death.

8.

Evening.

The inn - The Golden Anchor - was warm and comfortable. Grey had arranged for the king to be lodged in the largest room. The food was better than tolerable, although more than one guest suspected that the beef they served was really horsemeat. A couple of fires crackled at either end of the room. A few patrons, sitting away from the hearths, were wrapped in furs and drank steaming cups of mulled wine. More than one grumble could be heard when the door creaked opened to let in the biting draught.

The two would-be merchants were ensconced in the corner, minding their own business so to speak, as an oil lamp murmured above their heads. A couple of the king's bodyguards sat on a nearby table, sipping watered-down ale. Remaining painfully sober as they carried out their duties.

"I will be setting off at first light. But everything is in place. I have briefed the garrison commander, who will brief his officers tomorrow. I've been assured that construction on the false walls will be completed by dusk. Amerigo has confirmed that de Charny will send a few men in advance to deliver up the first instalment of his payment. And de Charny will be in possession of the second instalment," Sir Hugh Grey explained to the king.

"Good. It is not an insignificant sum, even after we reward Amerigo for his loyalty. Or rather treachery. It will certainly be enough to silence the yapping of a banker or two for the next couple of months. Defeating de Charny will prove even more priceless, however," Edward replied, already drafting the proclamation in his head, as he informed the populace about his famous victory to ring in the new year.

A squeal of laughter also rang out as Sir John Foxwist, sitting at a table with Sir Robert Seton, slapped the rump of a buxom serving girl.

"His wife would probably expect such behaviour, but I imagine that Foxwist's mistress might bridle at his unfaithfulness," Edward exclaimed, smiling into his winecup. The king couldn't quite remember if he had bedded the nobleman's current mistress or not. His plain-looking wife would certainly be free from his sovereign's advances, though.

Edward lifted his cup at a fellow at the counter, who raised his own cup in response. The king, pretending to be a humble merchant, had met the man, one Matthew Dugdale, the previous evening. He smirked, as he recalled the conversation with his lowly subject:

"You are over from England?" the grey bearded silversmith, who had moved to Calais from Kent, asked, as the strangers warmed themselves by the fire.

"Yes. Just attending to some business."

"Where do you hail from?"

"Windsor, although I also spend some of my time in London."

"Do you live close to King Edward?"

"You could say that. What do you think of the king and his reign?"

"He's certainly a better ruler than his father, which granted isn't a mountain to climb. I can remember a time when the French raided the Kent coast with impunity. But we've given the bully a bloody nose and he thinks twice about showing his face. Better to be a warmonger than a coward, I say. The English need not pay homage to anyone. Nor do I want anyone to pay homage to us. I'd like to pay less in taxes though. But who wouldn't? Have you ever seen the king in the flesh during your time in Windsor?"

"Once or twice. He stands about as tall as I am, more or less, but his hair is shorter and less bedraggled. Rumour is that he doesn't smile much, unless he is in the saddle fighting or jousting - or drinking. But let me put a smile on your face now and buy you an ale. Call it a tax rebate."

There were fewer merchants, fewer costly furs and more rumps being slapped at The Rusty Nail on the other side of town. Candles rather than oil lamps flickered. The smattering of sawdust covering the floor did little to disguise the old and fresh stains. The prince wasn't boarding at the establishment. He had asked Gower if they could visit a tavern filled with "commoners". Owain recommended The Rusty Nail.

"I drink there. And you can't get much more common than that, eh? They serve up horsemeat as beef, if you're lucky. God only knows what meat they put in their stew, which is more of a soup. It could be dog or cat, on a good day."

Rather than wealthy visitors to the port, the tavern was largely populated with locals from the less genteel part of town. They often sat according to their professions, with different guilds and trade such as joiners, dockers and stonemasons sitting together. Body heat helped keep the patrons warm. Unfortunately, body heat was accompanied by body odour.

The prince sat in the far corner on a rickety table with Gower. A few knights, who served under the prince, were spread throughout the large tavern, which after the lean years of the pestilence was now busy once more. Christmas had been celebrated with great gusto, as attested by the vomit and blood marking the flagstones outside afterwards. The strangers were eyed with suspicion or antipathy by the locals, especially as the more attractive serving girls were drawn to attending to the handsome newcomers who were not without funds.

The man-at-arms had promised that he would serve alongside the prince once more in the forthcoming engagement, although he asked for Sir Hugh Grey's permission first. Grey allowed for Gower to remain in Calais, indeed after a moment or two's thought he encouraged it. Not only did he appreciate the soldier's need to make money - as the prince had offered him a handsome wage to fight under his banner - but he also approved of the decision for another reason.

"It is probably for the best that we temporarily part ways, William. It will narrow the odds in relation to ensuring that one of us makes it back for Eleanor."

For a moment Gower experienced the bittersweet image of Eleanor framed in his mind eye. Even through the stench of the dung outside he could smell her perfume. He thought Eleanor was at her most beautiful in the sweet repose of when she was reading a book, or when she grinned riding her sable mare, Athena, with her auburn hair unfurled in the breeze. He felt both a pang of attraction and loss when Grey mentioned her name.

The floorboards may have been as uneven as the table. An expanding puddle of ale sat between the two men as they discussed the imminent clash of arms.

"Part of the reason we are here, I believe, is that my father wants to test the mettle of the Order of the Garter. We were not formed just to attend mass and pray in the chapel in Windsor… It's a bold plan, but as Ovid said, fortune favours the bold," the well-read prince remarked.

"Aye, although I'm unsure how many times your Ovid faced a French army three times or more the size of his own," Gower drolly countered.

"The king has one eye on the history books and chronicles. He wants people to think well of him in a hundred years, to be perhaps known as the hammer of the French in the same way that his grandfather is regarded as the hammer of the Scots. My father has plans for his fame to outlive himself. Perhaps I do too."

The man-at-arms considered how he could barely afford to plan for tomorrow. He didn't want to look beyond the next enemy standing in front of him, that needed cutting down. He would have also swapped a hundred poems and chronicles dedicated to him for Eleanor agreeing to be his wife.

"I'll settle for a purse full of coins than a life full of fame," Gower replied, whilst rubbing his jaw and feeling his burgeoning beard. Although the soldier was not usually prone to superstition, he promised that he would wait till after the encounter with the French before shaving. Or he may have just been being lazy rather than superstitious.

The prince caught the eye of a serving girl, beckoned her over and ordered a couple more drinks, furnishing the young woman with a coin for herself as a thank you.

"You're a prince among men, to be sure," Maggie Tunbridge proclaimed, fending off the urge to bite the coin to make sure it was real. The redhead had plump, freckled cheeks and even plumper breasts. Full lips, and a fuller figure. An inviting smile and a nice and naughty glint in her eye made her popular with patrons. Maggie wore a wooden cross around her neck, which she clutched when she prayed at night, kneeling next to her bed. The only time she had failed to say her prayers in the past two years her uncle had died the following day from the pestilence. Blessedly, she had not suffered any further bereavements.

"God is punishing us," her brother had said, when speaking about the plague.

"God isn't that vengeful," Maggie had replied, either innocently, wisely, faithfully or naively.

The prince had heard that serving girls from taverns were vigorous in bed, drunk or sober - and duly spoke to Maggie with a glint in his own eye. He had also heard that they were just as likely to steal one's purse as opposed to one's heart. Despite the chilly weather the woman still wore a low-cut dress, which showed off her assets. Aye, the customers duly appreciated the wench.

"Will you be paying us a visit tomorrow night?" the serving girl added.

"I'll be engaged tomorrow evening, I'm afraid. But perhaps we will have one more chance to have a drink here - and celebrate - before we journey back to England. I will make sure to buy you a drink or three as well," the prince remarked, charmingly.

"I can't let you buy me too many. You might want to take advantage of me."

"Only if you want me too."

The serving girl let out a laugh, blushes masking her freckles. The prince laughed too. The nobleman had spent enough time around soldiers not to blanch at a bawdy sense of a humour. He was also comfortable around a commoner's less than polished manners - and the circadian noises they sometimes emitted. During his stay in the town, he had unobtrusively taken note at the conversation and comments of his future subjects, often smiling as he did so.

"I could shit for England when I suffered a bout of the bloody flux. At the time I would have preferred to get lanced in the stomach at a tournament than suffer the wrenching guts ache I did. Even my marriage didn't cause me so much pain... I know that taxes are bad at the moment - and they'll probably get worse - but I heard from a Frenchman that they were worse when he lived in Calais. The French exchequer raped them as much as whores, or choir boys. Death and taxes seem more inevitable than ever these days..."

"There are some advantages to not being the heir to the throne, no?" Gower said, with a raised eyebrow, amused to see the shy youth he had known having turned into a man.

"I'm just getting to know my people. Especially the pretty ones, who will get down on their knees and pay me homage."

"As she said, you are a prince among men, your highness."

Edward laughed and raised his cup to his friend in a toast.

"I hear that you have found yourself a veritable princess have you not, William?"

"I sometimes wish that Owain could only speak in his native tongue. It will be time for you to find your own wife too, will it not?"

"No. I do not wish to relinquish my freedom and happiness quite yet. Marriage will be a contract, or business deal, for me. Or a life sentence. Unfortunately, it is unlikely that the pope, whether it's the one housed in Rome or Avignon, will allow me to keep the receipt and trade in my chattel for another. Princesses tend to be uglier than a leper, or Welshwoman. But I will duly exercise my royal prerogative and take a mistress, when I take a wife. They are two sides of the same coin, I warrant. But let's not hope it's a devalued coin, when I come to marry. But do not think that I do not know that you are deflecting and parrying, William. Tell me about your prospective wife."

"I dare say I have found the right woman. I just worry that she has not found the right man. Eleanor deserves someone worthier, with better prospects."

Before the prince could protest and argue that there were few worthier souls than the man-at-arms, he was cut off by a stranger approaching.

"You need to move. This is my table."

Before travelling to Calais, under the cloak of anonymity, the prince promised himself that he would aim to tup a comely serving girl, as well as take part in a tavern brawl. He was about to get his wish.

CALAIS

9.

The stonemason's features were as hard as the gargoyle figure he had worked next to that day, and just as ugly. Tom Rudge was not in a mood to be trifled with. He wanted a drink (or several) and he wanted the table that he usually sat at with his companions. He wore a besmirched leather jerkin over a thick, woollen shirt. An awl, hammer and chisel hung down from his belt. A clump of matted black hair sat on his head, which looked like it hadn't been washed since before the pestilence. Not even Hercules could have mustered the strength to run a comb through it. It would have been one too many labours. The brawny stonemason, who had moved to Calais from Cumbria, possessed a high forehead and pronounced lower lip. He sometimes appeared gormless. Looks are not always deceiving.

A half a dozen or so fellow stonemasons from his guild stood behind Rudge in a loose horseshoe. They were similarly attired and armed with the tools of their trade. The cold, thirsty labourers appeared similarly aggrieved that someone was sitting in the corner of the tavern that they deemed belonged to them.

The prince got to his feet, experiencing a heady mix of fear and excitement. Gower quickly stood by him. The man-at-arms imagined that the king wouldn't look too kindly on anyone who allowed his son to come to harm, as much as the prince seemed keen on putting himself in harm's way.

"This is our spot!" Rudge added, before snorting and spitting on the floor.

"Not tonight," the prince calmly but determinedly replied, in a slightly less guttural accent. "The French used to occupy this port. What do you think the king would say if he was instructed to give it back?"

The prince here smirked, thinking how he had nearly said "my father" rather than "the king".

"The king is an arse wipe! I couldn't care less for him," Rudge spat back, taking a step forward towards the irksome stranger. The stonemason believed that he had the numbers to settle any quarrel.

Either his opponent would back down, or he would beat him to a pulp and toss him out of the tavern like a ragdoll.

"I'm tempted to take that insult personally. You wouldn't be standing here, you piece of shit hanging off an arse wipe, if it wasn't for the king's valour," the prince replied, somewhat less calmly, taking a step forward too.

Gower rolled his eyes and sighed, before cracking his knuckles as he balled his hand into a fist.

Rudge was the first to throw a punch, but it failed to land. The prince, who hoped to provoke the stonemason and was expecting the attack, had honed his reflexes during many a melee. He swiftly leaned back, letting Rudge's fist brush past his face, before leaning forward and jabbing his opponent square in the pate, splitting open his already flattened nose. Rudge staggered backwards into the arms of his apprentice.

Alfred Chard, a burly stonemason with a cauliflower ears and straw-coloured hair, looked to blindside the prince but before he could free the chisel from his belt Gower tossed the contents of his tankard into his face and then smashed the pewter receptacle across his skull, denting the rim in the process.

The stonemasons let out some garbled curses and clenched their fists. Ready. Willing. Able. "The king loves all his subjects, though there are some rogues and miscreants that he deservedly loves less."

The noblemen thought nothing of attacking their opponents from behind. And The Rusty Nail was not known for being a paragon of chivalry. Sir John Beauchamp dragged one unsuspecting stonemason to the floor and unceremoniously stamped on his head, as if hammering a tent peg into the ground. Sir John Montagu punched an opponent in the kidneys, before turning him around and elbowing him - shattering the poor man's left cheekbone. The assault was as fast as it was ferocious.

Maggie Tunbridge seemed veritably aroused by the handsome stranger's show of strength. Her hand clutched her cross, perhaps in a gesture of praying for him. She hoped that Tom Rudge would somehow injure his hands so he would be unable to grope her. The spectators similarly enjoyed the show, especially as many had been victims of Rudge's bullying before. More than one customer concluded that the head of the guild had it coming.

"Who were they?" a local asked afterwards, in reference to the newcomers.

"D'you know, I thought one of them looked like Prince Edward. I saw him once at a tournament in Winchester," his companion replied.

"You've had one too many drinks, I think. But it's your round so go up and get us some more."

Arms flailed. A couple of teeth rattled across the floorboards like waywardly thrown dice. But the contest, if it could be called as such, was over almost as soon as it commenced. Rudge and his party were left groaning on their backs.

The landlord's mouth was agape in response to the altercation, although his jaw dropped even further when the patron who had stood his ground against the troublesome guild handed over several coins, which covered his drinks and any damages caused during the scuffle. No one had ever tried to compensate the owner before. Aside from mumbling "thank you" he was lost for words.

The prince grinned, his teeth gleaming (which was, again, a rarity for a customer in the tavern). He almost wanted the group of stonemasons to get to their feet so he could continue the one-sided brawl.

"Let's hope that tomorrow night proves as easy and as enjoyable," he remarked, enthusiastically, to Gower, after downing the dregs of his ale.

If only, the man-at-arms thought.

10.

Lamps hung from the ceiling of the pavilion tent which the king himself had gifted to de Charny to aid him in his vital mission. Unfortunately, Philip had also sent the gift of a surfeit of noblemen, who believed they were somehow in command of the small army too. There had been a minor furore when senior men-at-arms had attempted to enter the tent and join the briefing. A sect of knights baulked at the lowly infantrymen sitting side by side with the aristocracy - and threatened to withdraw from the meeting. In order to quell the dispute and prevent further delays de Charny apologised to the men-at-arms and compensated them with some wine (but not too much) and delicacies from his personal stores. Most of the veteran soldiers who were ejected were worth ten of the self-glorifying young knights inside the tent.

Thankfully de Charny was too focused on the mission at hand to be overly distracted by the gaggle of aristocrats who surrounded him. Food was served. The preening noblemen settled down. Attendants and petty functionaries were ordered out of the tent. Some had seemed to be in competition with one another as to who could fuss over their master the most.

Geoffrey de Charny stood up and raised his hand to signify quiet. A gold cross hung around his neck, glinting in what little light there was. He wore a laundered linen shirt beneath a quilted, studded brown coat. "One's clothes should be as spotless as one's conscience," the Christian soldier had been known to say. Long, dark hair framed a pleasing face and piercing, intelligent eyes. The renowned knight appeared younger than his forty plus years. Soldiering had conditioned rather than broken his body. The third son of Jean de Charny, the nobleman had needed to make his own way in the world. He did so by turning himself into one of the foremost warriors of his age, earning money first through tournaments and then through the business of war. He had also made a name for himself as an author, having penned several tracts and books. He seldom spent a day idle. "He who does more is worth more," de

Charny professed. Life was a journey. The destination was heaven. Life should be devoted to constant improvement. Skill brought military prowess. Prowess brought victory on the battlefield. War was an honourable pursuit, approved of by God if one's enemies were impious. A knight could, or perhaps should, ultimately be a martyr. The knight's reputation for chivalry and charm preceded him, to the point where he felt he had to live-up to his reputation. All manner of people would ask him about his exploits and "chivalric code" - but the soldier had long grown bored rather than flattered by the attention. More than one lady had given the knight the token of a garter, hoping or expecting to receive something in return. More than one woman also hoped that the nobleman's wife might perish in the pestilence.

Although de Charny admired the English for some of their martial virtues, they were also an opponent who needed to be defeated. Calais belonged to the French - and France was the great light of the world, the apogee of civilisation and culture. The jewel of Christendom. When Philip invited the knight to lead the expedition, he did not need to be asked twice.

The Frenchman and Lombard had a common enemy, de Charny believed. Amerigo de Pavia was merely aligning himself with the greater power. Loyalty was a commodity which could be purchased, it seemed - although de Charny conversely told himself that he would not betray his homeland for all the wealth of Charlemagne.

He proceeded to inform and inspire his captains.

"...We have surprise on our side, as well as the greater numbers. But take nothing for granted. The English, if roused in time, will fight like lions. There will be a small garrison of hardened, professional veterans present. Most will be asleep. But not all. It is not only the soldiers you should be mindful of, however. If a blacksmith picks up a poker you should consider him a dangerous opponent. If you see a greybeard carrying a cane, do not discount that he has a blade on his person too. It will also be late. The drunks being thrown out of the taverns will not go gently into the night. This evening will be a bloody business, but we will triumph," de Charny posited. He wished to instil confidence in his men, but not overconfidence.

"The more defiant the vile English are the better, as far as I'm concerned," Charles de Jardun announced. "They deserve to be put to the sword. We should cut them out of the walls of the town like they were a cancer. How merciful was their king when he let the women and children of Calais starve?"

Sweat glazed the young count's face. He was already dressed in his armour, which he frequently boasted was made by the finest armourer in Castile. There was not a single dint or dent in his suit, which worried rather than reassured his commander. It would be the nineteen-year old's first engagement. His father, an honourable soldier who had served with de Charny during the Smyrna campaign, had fallen at Crécy. De Jardun's elder, childless brother had recently died from the pestilence. "Charles has inherited a significant estate," the king had told de Charny. "I would consider it a personal favour if you took him under your wing and included him in your party."

"Let us hope that the youth has inherited a spine from his father too," de Charny had replied, having once witnessed the peacock at court, brandishing a bejewelled sword and wearing a silk blouse.

The commander duly ignored the unwanted comment from the count and continued his briefing.

"Guy here will lead an advance party of a few mounted troops into the town. They will rendezvous with our contact inside Calais and pay him the first instalment of his fee. He will then proceed to raise our banner as a signal to advance, lower the drawbridge and open the gate to the bulk of our forces."

The aristocrats, drawn from many of the noblest families in France, briefly turned their attention towards Guy Mabrice, seated next de Charny. A few inwardly bridled at not being given the responsibility and honour of commanding the vanguard. The lieutenant was part of the nobility, being the youngest son of unremarkable stock, but his face would never fit at court. Mabrice had a dusky complexion, even in winter, which led some to question his ancestry. More than one of the knights in the tent had sneeringly commented that Mabrice looked "Moorish". Due to several years spent soldiering, Mabrice had adopted the coarse sense of humour and manners of the common soldiers he served with - and preferred to drink with. Like de Charny, he had initially made a name for himself at tournaments. At seventeen years old he had been invited to make-up the numbers in a melee, just outside of Nantes. Yet he triumphed, defeating far more experienced soldiers. He soon schooled himself in horsemanship - and within a couple of years he was rarely bested in the joust. Having come to the attention of de Charny, the knight asked Mabrice to join him on his campaign against the Turks. He fought well, having saved his commander's life on more than one occasion. The young man knew when to listen and when to speak. He was fearless but not reckless. Proud but not vainglorious. The commander also admired his lieutenant for his devotion to his family. He sent most of the money he earned back home. His father's estate was often on the brink of ruin, due to high taxes - as well as the other disease of the age.

Although de Charny knew that Mabrice's promotion would breed shards of envy and resentment, hurt feelings were less important than dead bodies. He knew that Oudart de Renti would feel slighted - but he would probably still claim he was in charge of the advance party. Eustace de Ribbemont might feel aggrieved too at being overlooked. But de Charny trusted his lieutenant to carry out his orders - and not let personal glory intrude upon the greater good. The commander would also ensure that a cadre of reliable men accompanied the two strongboxes, containing the Lombard's fee. The sum was sufficient to tempt even the wealthiest of knights.

"Once we are inside the town, we need to overwhelm the nearby barracks and occupy the battlements. I will lead a small force and look to open the Boulogne Gate, where a secondary force will be waiting to enter. Securing the town will only be half the battle, however," de Charny warned, his tone calm and authoritative. "We must maintain the discipline of our own soldiers. Lead by example. If gold should rust, what will lead do? We do not want to earn an ill report. I will task some of you with protecting the churches. I will not permit our places of worship to be despoiled. Any looting or sacrilegious acts will be stringently punished. Any damage in general we cause to the town will be an act of self-harm, as we will inherit the damage."

Soldiers, even or especially those fighting in the name of a righteous cause, could be prone to sin.

The French commander had secured the attention and respect of many in the tent, albeit de Charny pursed his lips and stared at Augustus de Corbie with thinly veiled contempt as the young aristocrat kept turning towards an upturned silver tray on the table next to him. He constantly adjusted his fringe, in between combing his beard.

"You are captains of France. You should duly feel a sense of pride and honour. But you should also feel a sense of responsibility towards the men you command," de Charny added, thinking how it was unlikely that de Corbie's men would fight for him. There were scores of young men outside, looking to the noblemen to lead them. Many would be widowers and orphans due to the pestilence. Few appeared as if they felt lucky to be alive, though, de Charny mused.

It was a slight regret that he was taking the town by subterfuge, rather than through a pitched battle, the Frenchman also mused, later that evening. Part of the soldier wanted to face the English king in battle, having not been present at Crécy. He respected his enemy. Several years ago, de Charny was captured by the English at the Battle of Morlaix. The French knight was taken across the Channel. He resided in Goodrich Castle under the charge of Richard Talbot. His captor became his friend (the baron eventually gave the Frenchman leave to return to his homeland and raise the money for his ransom), and de Charny would often enquire about the customs of England and the character of the king, learning the language of his opponent as he did so. Edward had become an enigmatic and imposing figure, ever since he had burst into his mother and Roger Mortimer's chamber and taken his kingdom back at the age of seventeen.

"Edward has long eclipsed his father, which admittedly isn't the greatest of achievements," Talbot commented. "He is just and thoughtful, although he can be quick to anger if irritated, especially when suffering a visit from an official telling him that parliament is unwilling to raise taxes again. But he is not without a sense of humour, as well as a temper. Your king would do well to learn from Edward and be able to share a joke and drink with his subjects... The peasants are not revolting. Well, some of them are... The king is every inch a formidable warrior, his grandfather's son. Edward leads from the front rank - and his men follow him for that fact. He has a grasp of logistics, surrounds himself with soldiers rather than sycophants and knows that no one is entitled to victory. Victory must be earned… There are few who can best him with a blade or lance… He is devoted to his wife, even more than he is to his stable of mistresses…"

"'Tis a shame, Guy, that we will not have the opportunity to face the king and his army," de Charny remarked to his lieutenant, after the briefing. "I would have liked to test myself against the pride of the English. I pity the messenger who will have to deliver the news concerning the fall of Calais to Edward."

"Aye," Mabrice replied, thinking how he would have liked to test himself against the king's son. The prince had won his reputation at Crécy. The Frenchman would have liked to help him lose it at Calais.

11.

The party ploughed on, through the mizzle and glutinous mud, led by Sir Hugh Grey and Richard Maldon, commanding half the company of longbowmen. The chill wind pierced them like bodkin-tipped shafts. They had risen early, with heavy heads and leaden-lidded eyes. But the vintenar had ensured that they set off with full-bellies and full arrow bags. Thankfully the direction they were heading was opposite to de Charny's approaching force.

"What's the plan?" one of Maldon's men had asked his captain that morning.

"To do what I fucking tell you to do and stop asking questions. You get paid for killing, not thinking," Maldon replied, his mood as black as the pre-dawn sky.

France, like England, was in a state of disrepair after the harrowing of the pestilence. The country had suffered as much, or even more, than Grey's homeland. The spymaster could almost feel sorry for his enemy. Almost. A steeple was missing from a church in the distance. Hedgerows were overgrown, as unruly as an ageing whore's wig. Frozen, maggot infested carrion littered fallow fields. Villages were half-empty. Hollowed out faces had gawped at the party of archers who passed by. The nobleman had spoken to them in French, wishing to deceive them into believing that the soldiers were their countrymen. But the pallid villagers appeared either too weary or defeated to care.

The pestilence had been unforgiving, or was it God who had proved unforgiving - or vengeful? At best the Almighty could have been described as indifferent. An absent landlord.

As indifferent as Grey could be about a great many things he had been pleased to see the Welsh archer again, who had saved his life during the carnage at Crécy. He wryly smiled as the roguish soldier reported on his litany of losses at the gaming table.

"You may have to face the awful truth, Owain. You are about as adept at dice as a one-armed man is at shooting a bow," Grey exclaimed, whilst fastidiously brushing some flecks of mud from his russet-coloured cloak, fastened together with a silver brooch in the shape of a quill.

"My luck can only change," the Welshman piped back, riddled with optimism like a pox.

"Aye, it can get even worse. The men must be queuing up in line to play you. You will soon be running up debts to rival the crown. You may not be able to throw dice, but the main thing is you can still shoot," Grey said, thinking that was the central qualification for joining Maldon's company. The vintenar had spared more than one killer from the gallows by recruiting him into his company, due to the man's prowess with a bow. The latest that Maldon had told Grey about was one Luke Palmer, a Suffolk poacher who had butchered his wife for her infidelities one drunken evening.

"If every man committed murder in reply for a wife being unfaithful then the gallows would be endlessly creaking from some fellow swinging from them, I warrant," Richard Maldon added.

"You have done well to give these souls a second chance, Richard. You have made honest men out of them," Grey asserted.

"I dare say they're not too honest. They're men after all. But they'll stand their ground and let loose half a dozen arrows before a French crossbowman can pick the garlic out of his teeth."

The rain fell harder, like tiny needles of ice, and the ground grew softer. The party trudged on, half on them dwelling on what might unfold during their mission, with the other half imagining what they might spend their bonus on.

Maldon, after dropping back to check on his men, broke into a brief canter and joined the nobleman.

"Don't lend him any money. You'll never see it again. He's veritably throwing his life away," the vintenar said, referring to the Welshman who he liked, but could feel exasperated by.

"Ain't we all throwing our lives away, in one way or another?" Owain countered, with a shrug.

"The knave has a point," Grey stated, unable to suppress a grin.

It was now time for the Welsh bowman to drop back and converse with the men behind, hoping that someone would allow him to use the stake of an unpaid bonus to join the next game of dice.

The two men at the vanguard of the group rode on in silence. Grey glanced at his fellow widower. The longbowman had a broken nose and scarred chin, but he had killed far more of the enemy than the enemy had wounded him over the years. Maldon's countenance was as frozen as the birch trees occasionally lining the track. He noticed the archer's pronounced Adam's apple and thought about how one could endlessly choke upon grief. But one could never wholly swallow it and make it disappear. Maldon appeared both numb and pained. His cheeks had hollowed out since last encountering the soldier. His hair was greyer, his smile flatter. The spymaster recognised his companion's haunted expression. He had witnessed it plenty of times in the mirror over the years. Michiel Auclair, the nobleman's old friend, had once tried to console him by arguing that it was better to have loved and lost than not to have loved at all. But the widower wasn't so sure.

Rain thrummed against the murky windowpane. Inside, father and son feasted on some mutton chops, washed down with the king's favourite ale which he had brought over from England. Attendants and advisers had been shooed out of the chamber like stray cats.

The elder Edward smiled, with more than a dash of paternal pride, as he recalled how one of his knights had loyally reported on the events of yesternight. The king, no stranger to youthful exuberance, had instructed the prince to keep his head down and not draw attention to himself. But he could forgive his son's disobedience - partly because he had acquitted himself well and put down his opponent. Winning can absolve a multitude of sins.

But the enemy would prove more skilled and sober this evening. The king had arranged a mass that morning to prepare his knights. It was always wise to try to recruit God to your cause. He had also compelled members of the Order of the Garter and others to take confession.

"You will all be able to move quicker in your armour if unburdened by the weight of your sins."

The prince solemnly confessed some imaginary sins when dealing with the simpering, fragrant priest. His real sins and impure thoughts would steadfastly remain between him and the Almighty, he resolved. After surviving the fighting at Crécy, illness during the siege of Calais and, touch wood, escaping the great mortality, the prince sometimes believed that God had spared him for a reason. A divine purpose. The prince would one day become king - and the king would unite the crowns of England and France, if his father hadn't already done so. Perhaps he would then hear the call to travel on a crusade to the Holy Land. The Christian soldier would often visit the chapel in Windsor when it was empty. He would pray to God and St George. Mourn those lost to the pestilence and talk to his beloved sister. He still could picture her heart-shaped face and hear her girlish laughter. The body of Princess Joan had never been brought back. They had never buried her. The devout prince would often ask the Almighty to spare his mother and father, as well as his younger brother, John. It is best that you keep the boy here in this world. Otherwise, he will only annoy you and the angels with his incessant talking.

"You will command the reserve later. Hopefully we will not have need of you, but even the best laid plans will not survive contact with the enemy. Be ready. History will report a famous victory against a renowned opponent - and not just because I will endeavour to compose the history myself. Sharpen your sword later, if you have not already done so. Ensure that even if the blade freezes up if does not get stuck in its scabbard. Check your armour and the straps on your shield. I wouldn't forgive myself if anything happened to you, son. Far more importantly, your mother would never forgive me. I fear her wrath more than de Charny's. Young John wouldn't forgive me either. Your brother may idolise you more than he does me. But nobody's perfect. The boy is showing remarkable intelligence and ambition, even at an early age. I suspect that he doesn't want to rule the world, just lease it and charge others rent."

The prince initially nodded dutifully in response to his father, before smiling fondly as he pictured his younger, devoted sibling. John, who had yet to reach ten years of age, would sometimes gaze at his elder brother in wonder, as if he were the brightest star in firmament. He would watch him train and hang on his every word as the famed warrior recounted tales from his campaigns and tournaments.

The once fertile fields looked like an immense brown scab, covering a wound which would never heal. The trees appeared as emaciated and diseased as the peasantry living in the nearby village.

Creton was frustrated by the progress, or lack thereof, they were making. He instructed Bernard Murat, who oversaw the spymaster's retinue of enforcers, to threaten and punish any errant malingerers. The cart which carried both supplies and the strongbox containing Sir Robert Seton's fee was frequently getting bogged down in the mud.

Murat's expression became as inhospitable as the weather. He barked out orders and boxed more than one ear in. Creton had recently promoted the former soldier. He didn't ask questions or hesitate when carrying out his duties, which a man with a sense of honour or conscience might have if serving under Creton. The mercenary was proficient with a crossbow, sword and axe. He could lead, torture and kill. The Breton had lost his wife and four children to the pestilence, which Creton was secretly pleased about as it meant that the bodyguard could now devote himself to his work. Creton believed that men were inclined to sin, indolence and bestial behaviour. They needed discipline and a greater figure to fear than God to instil a sense of purpose in them. Fear of punishment in this life is usually a better incentive than the promise of a reward in the next, he calculated.

Creton's "hounds" as he called them were a far from pleasant looking bunch - but they were all the more intimidating for it. Jean Gien wore a patch over his left eye, from having it gouged out during an altercation in a tavern over the issue of a drinking companion trying to duck out of buying a round. Olivier Jarnac, a heavyset veteran, possessed a stump where his right hand used to be, thanks to an English axe. What he lacked in dexterity he more than made for in brutality. Henri Thian, a former horse thief from Picardy, boasted how he had a rule that he would never rape a Frenchwoman, but any other "mares" were fair game.

The spymaster - a somewhat lapsed Catholic - knew that it was not only soldiers who could resemble beasts, however. Creton had witnessed noblemen and monarchs up close. He had seen kings in the flesh, God's semi-divine representatives on earth, behave like satyrs - priapic and perverted. Drunk. Lustful. Making fools of themselves over pox-ridden harlots. Or actresses. They would drool and their eyes would bulge like buboes, before or after they rutted like stoats. Disgusting and deplorable, Creton thought, with all the judgement of an un-lapsed Catholic.

"Do you trust this Englishman?" Murat asked, as he re-joined his employer at the head of the column.

"As much as one can trust anyone. I trust him to be self-serving and greedy. He has also proved to be reliable in the past," Creton posited. Seton's intelligence had helped expose French traitors, although the agents had sadly evaded capture. The English nobleman, intimate with Edward's inner circle, had also provided accurate information pertaining to enemy troop numbers and their deployment. The pestilence and French reticence - or martial cowardice - meant that they were unable to capitalise on the intelligence coup, though. The aristocrat, often living at court in Windsor, had also been able to feed through morsels of tasty gossip to Creton, who in turn served them up to the French king for his amusement and delectation.

But it seemed that Seton was about to outdo himself with the treasure chest of correspondence he had appropriated. Edward would be injured by his own hand, or rather own handwriting. His authority and prestige would be diminished. The scandal and embarrassment might split his court in two. His creditors might turn off the tap. His people might deride him or at least consider him a laughingstock. Even the popes might be compelled to unite against the Edward and excommunicate him. Should de Charny succeed in his mission too this evening then it could be the beginning of the end of the English king and his cause. One could argue that the famed French knight was everything that Creton was not - noble, handsome, chivalrous - but the spy found himself wishing his counterpart well. He licked his lips at the prospect of their joint success. There was no such thing as spilling too much English blood.

"A spy's work is never done," his mentor, Fossat, had often proclaimed (it was one of many sage sayings that the official gifted his successor). But Creton had accumulated sufficient wealth and was in a position to retire and enjoy the fruits of his labours. Obtaining the letters from the English aristocrat would be his crowning glory. "The reward will be worth any risk," he conveyed to

Murat.

Creton would be unable to find peace, however, until he resolved the issue of Sir Hugh Grey. There had been times when the Frenchman's usually stony semblance had twitched upon people mentioning his name. Rivals at court would use Grey to humiliate and bait him. The Englishman's network in Paris seemed hydra headed. Every time his hounds would capture a French agent, rumours of two more operating in the city would come to his attention. Creton had become obsessed with knowing more about his enemy - and destroying him. The Frenchman had even purchased a portrait of the Englishman for a significant sum - and installed it in his study. The painting inspired him, fed his animus, reminding him of the debt his owed his opponent.

The cart was once more extracted from the mud and the party advanced. Creton's frustration was tempered by the promise of eventual success.

A scrawny fox, darting out from beneath an abandoned, broken wagon wheel caught his attention. Its matted, mangy fur was the colour of dried blood. The creature glanced back at the French spy, offering up a look of distrust rather than curiosity. The creature's mouth hung open, revealing a set of sharp, yellow teeth. Creton smiled to himself, imagining how the famished animal wouldn't think twice in chewing off a baby's face.

CALAIS

12.

Dusk.

The inviting glow on the horizon was not reflected in the inhospitable temperature, Creton thought as he arrived at the abandoned, destitute farm. He never cared much for anything which could be judged picturesque. God could be discerned and measured in a profit and loss column rather than a sunset. Shutters were hanging on for dear life, the chimney was half missing and vines seemed to be strangling the cottage in the background. Only the weeds seemed to have flourished in the winter. The spymaster now understood why Seton had decided to host their meeting in the barn on the remote property.

A couple of horses were tethered to a rail by the side of the run-down wooden structure. Finally, they had arrived. Finally, he would get his hands on the prize.

Creton instructed Murat and three other men to accompany him inside. Two of them were charged with carrying the strongbox containing the Englishman's payment. The rest of the hounds were instructed to remain outside. Many dismounted and decided to stretch their legs and stamp their feet. Some retrieved wineskins or fished out what little food they had left.

Through the narrow cracks of the small door, which was set within the barn's larger entrance, Creton could see that his host had lit a couple of fires to help illuminate and warm the space. The barn would have held grain or other crops when part of a working farm. It was spacious and could have housed his men and most of their horses - but the spy would leave his retinue outside. He desired privacy. The barn would be infused with the stench of his hounds and their horses should he permit them to congregate inside.

The four French soldiers were met by three English ones - and a Welshman. But the contest was no contest, as their arrows were already nocked upon their bows. Before the confused hounds could lay down the strongbox or draw their weapons the twang of bowstrings sounded in the air. It was the last noise they would hear, along with the blare of a trumpet, as abrasive as the sound of the last judgement.

The clarion call was a signal for Maldon's archers to unleash their volley of missiles from behind a hedgerow running parallel to the barn. The arrows swarmed through the air and rained down on the exposed, unarmoured enemy - slaughtering man and beast alike. Although in a couple of instances the beasts killed their riders, as they reared up or bolted, trampling riders underfoot. Screams curdled the air, howling more loudly than the wind, which occasionally slammed against the side of the barn. Bodkin and broad headed arrows thudded into leather, mail, wool and flesh. Five deadly waves of shafts, their white feathers gleaming in the dying rays of the sun, soared through the air and made pincushions of their ambushed opponents within a minute. Maldon then ordered a half a dozen of his men to draw their short swords and race towards the defeated opponents. The injured were swiftly turned into the dead, with a few sluicing sounds accompanying the mellow sunset.

All was not well. Creton heard the screams of his men, among the screeching of the horses, but they were mere background noise to the voice inside his head, trying to collect his thoughts. He duly recognised the well-attired figure in front of him from the portrait hanging in his study. What colour there was in the official's face drained away, like piss spiralling down a gutter. The spy had been deceived. It felt like someone had skewered him with a pike and was twisting his intestines around it.

Sir Hugh Grey stood in between a couple of fires. Rusting farming tools sat in the corner next to a dusty milking stool. A few empty sacks and a half- eaten mouse occupied the other far corner. Grey had used the cottage over the years as a safehouse for agents who needed to evade the authorities. The pestilence had killed the tenants, who had acted under the Englishman's direction, the previous year. Grey had reached the property early, to plan out his ambush with Maldon and wait for their quarry. He instructed for a couple of fires to be lit. He didn't want any of the bowmen's fingers to be numb when the enemy arrived. So, the spy waited, as patient as a soldier.

"You were expecting to meet Sir Robert. Sorry to disappoint you," Grey remarked in French, with a polite and playful smile. His tone was the soul of civility. "You must recognise me from my portrait. I made sure that my friend received a good price from you, when I discovered from an intermediary that you were interested in procuring the painting. I think I should be flattered that you wanted it. I am not sure I am, though. You were also hoping that I was dead, I imagine. Again, sorry to disappoint you. You crossed a line by attempting to assassinate myself and my household, Raymon. One of us had to die. As loathsome as I can be - none of us are free from sin in this world - I still preferred it to be you. Sir Robert has long been in my service. He played the embittered and impoverished knight, ripe to betray king and country. To prove his bona fides I furnished him with nuggets of intelligence to pass on to you. Mere chicken feed, so to speak. I ensured that any agent he gave up was safely ensconced in England beforehand. I knew that the prize of the cache of letters would draw you out, like a tic. It came from a credible source, for a credible fee. I would not be entirely surprised if such correspondence did exist in earnest. I may have fallen for the same ruse, if you had dangled the same bait in front of me. As much as we may deal in deception, we spies would like some things to be true as well."

Creton appeared fatter and jowlier than Grey had envisioned him, although the Englishman was too courteous to mention it. His cassock was stretched across his pronounced paunch. His eyes seemed deep-set in his pudding-face and would express, at different times, shock, shrewdness, fear and malice throughout the encounter.

"The fat bastard looks like he's going to be sick, or that he's just found out he's a cuckold!" Owain remarked, leaning on his bow and smirking. The archer possessed scant pity for the man who had tried to murder his friend in his sleep.

Creton remained silent, crestfallen, as a couple of the English bowmen retrieved the strongbox and placed it in front of the nobleman. He glanced down at the fallen Murat. He seemed unhappy to be dead, his mouth twisted in a macabre frown. The soldier would have at least wanted to go down fighting. But life didn't resemble The Song of Roland. There is no great author, or divine hand, behind events. The Frenchman realised that there was no one coming to save him. Should he be in his counterpart's position, he would ruthlessly torture and then execute his prisoner. But the French spy clung to the hope that he had one last card to play. His mouth was dry, his voice croaky, but Creton grew in confidence as he eventually raised his head and spoke:

"I will not insult your intelligence and say that I had nothing to do with the attempt on your life. But you need to understand that I was only following orders. We are participants in the same game. We know the rules, or lack of rules. We both know that there is little honour between even monarchs and popes. Why should we expect honour between spies? The order to kill you was never anything personal, Sir Hugh. It just seems that the wheel of fortune has turned once more."

"The portrait you purchased of me and boasts to figures at court that you would take your revenge may beg to differ. I am not here on official business. This is entirely a personal matter now. Not even Saint George could intercede for you. God may happily forgive me should I torture you in the same fashion that you tortured my dear friend Michiel Auclair. The wheel of fortune is about to stop turning, or come off, for you," Grey replied, his voice and features hardening.

"I could prove an asset to you. I have enemies at court, who are also enemies of King Edward and England. There is a plan to take Calais. A captain, one Amerigo de Pavia, has accepted a bribe. I can give you the details. There may be time to still save the port. I am also not without funds. I can reward both you and your men should you spare my life. I know that you are not without honour, Sir Hugh. You are a nobleman and Christian," Creton said, words tumbling out of his mouth like broken teeth. Breathless. Desperate. He would not blame the Englishman if he thought he was lying about the plot to seize Calais. The French spy had heard countless confessions over the years where prisoners would say anything to delay the inevitable.

"He talks too much. Can't we just slit the devil's throat and return home? I'd rather see in the new year listening to some drinking songs than hear this cocksucker gab on," Owain said, drawing his knife and suppressing a yawn.

"No, please. Wait. Listen. I still have a piece of intelligence that you will want to trade, to spare my life for," Creton exclaimed, raising the palm of his hands in a plea for peace and patience.

CALAIS

The English spymaster had already considered the value of using Creton as an asset. But the Frenchman could be trusted about as much as a Turk - and he would be of greater value dead. As much as he appreciated Owain's willingness to execute the prisoner, Grey drew his own blade and took a step forward. But he soon stopped - and the sword hung limply in his hand after the Frenchman spoke.

"I know the name of the man who murdered your family. Grace and Beatrice. I will tell you in exchange for my life."

It was the Englishman's turn to become momentarily speechless. Shocked. The nobleman had turned himself into an assassin and spy, all those years ago, in order to fulfil his vow to avenge his wife's death. His daughter's death. The French raid on the village where his family was residing had been the beginning, or end, of it all for the grief-stricken aristocrat. Part of him felt like cutting Creton's throat, just for the sacrilege of him mentioning their names. But part of him had to spare his enemy. To hear his confession first. To know the truth…

Voices could be heard from outside as silence hung in the air inside the barn, as a group of soldiers rummaged through the pockets of their enemy and revelled in their easy victory.

"God's blood, we've had a good day's work. What will you spend your share on?" one John Trussell, a former poacher from Suffolk, pronounced, whilst yanking a broad headed arrow out of a scrawny neck.

"A clean whore, who can talk filth," Matthew Wyard chimed in immediately, as if the bowman from Essex had already long since considered the question. "And you?"

"The extra coin will hopefully buy me some peace and quiet from my wife for a month or two. It'll be priceless," Thomas Smith replied, not joking half as much as his companions thought he was.

"I intend to drink myself stupid," John "Ox" Bull declared, one of ten brothers from Norfolk, who had recently married a not so distant cousin.

"Well, that won't take long," Trussell declared, to a chorus of laughter, before sawing off a French finger to pocket a silver ring.

Owain had never seen the aristocrat appear so perturbed. The Welshman might have once considered it desirable for the

Englishman to be lost for words. He looked like he had seen a ghost. He had understood the words "Grace and Beatrice" during the Frenchman's speech.

The image of Grace scythed through his brain like a bolt of lightning. He suddenly felt nauseous, as queasy as a drunk. Although he had maintained his promise (to himself, his late wife and God) of fighting against the French, Grey had given up hope of ever finding the person responsible for butchering his wife and child.

"I would not blame you, of course, if you did not believe me," Creton added, ending the pregnant pause. "Why should you? But you would blame yourself if you did not hear me out. You would be right to ask the question, how do I know who is responsible? I know because the man who sanctioned the raid was my mentor, Edvard Fossat. You are aware that I served under Fossat and that he was responsible for the campaign against the English during the time of your family's murder. I once procured a list of the captains who headed up various raids. Fossat has long passed, but the man you are seeking could still be alive. I am willing to trade his name for my life."

Grey knew that he had it in his power to loosen Creton's tongue. He could easily torture the prisoner to force him to reveal the name. But he wanted his curiosity and appetite for revenge satisfied immediately.

"Give me the name," the Englishman stated, either as a demand or plea.

"Not until you give me your word that I will not die by your hand. I swear, my hand to God, that if you spare me then I will rescind any directive to assassinate you and your household," the Frenchman promised. Lying.

"You have my word that I will not kill you."

Creton nodded and smiled. Satisfied. Relieved. Should he survive this day, he vowed to himself that he would re-double his efforts to capture and kill the Englishman. The spy would be honest, however, and divulge the name of the agent. He might then serve as bait to apprehend Grey.

"Giles Albret."

The Englishman resembled a mathematician or philosopher,

either posing a problem to himself or solving one. Grey had heard the name before. He had read "Albret" on a list Frenchmen suspected of leading raids along the English coast. The spy didn't need to write the name down. He would remember it, as surely as he would his own.

A silence briefly hung in the air once more, before Grey gave the order for Owain to execute the prisoner.

"You promised that you would not kill me," Creton hastily protested, his voice and body trembling as the bowman marched towards him.

"I'm not going to kill you. My friend is," Grey replied, either curtly or nonchalantly.

Cold, unadulterated fear flooded Creton's being, to the point where he didn't even notice the warm piss running down his leg. He fell to his knees and let out a garbled appeal for mercy in English, but the Welshman wasn't in a merciful mood. His eyes bulged and heart raced in terror. Creton had witnessed such a look before, numerous times - but it was when he had served as an interrogator rather than a prisoner.

Owain grabbed a fistful of material of the Frenchman's cassock with one hand as he moved the point of his blade towards Creton's neck with the other. The spy clasped the brawny archer's arm. The gesture merely delayed rather than prevented the inevitable.

Creton recalled one of the adages of his mentor, as the tip of the sword pricked his neck.

"Death comes to everyone. Just make sure you outlive all your enemies first."

Dozens of other thoughts galloped through his mind, trampling the preceding thoughts underfoot. His pride smarted, perhaps as much as the burgeoning wound in his neck, as he took in the English aristocrat standing over him. Creton bared his teeth, in pain as well as hatred.

Sir Hugh Grey felt a certain amount of uneasiness at experiencing such satisfaction at the sight before him. He sighed, in either relief or weariness, as Creton took his last breath - blood bubbling out of his throat, just beneath his Adam's apple. The Englishman had once attended church twice a week when married to Grace. He enjoyed evensong and liked to re-draft in his head the sermons he heard, to make them more appealing and impactful. He had never shared the evangelical atheism of some of his fellow students at Oxford. He had considered himself a Christian. Could he do so now?

"I sometimes think that I am a pilgrim - but one heading towards the darkness rather than the light," he had confessed to Gower one evening, around Easter, as the friends shared a couple of vintages.

Grey maintained his agreement with Maldon and granted him half the contents of the strongbox to distribute to his company. He would use a portion of the rest to reward Constance for her service - and to compensate her for the inconvenience of nearly being murdered. The spy would be sure to remunerate Sir Robert Seton too. The nobleman would also set some of the money aside to pay a couple of his creditors. He had new, overdue payments to his tailor and wine merchant to settle.

All debts must come due, Grey believed. Creton had just paid for his sins. Albret would pay for his as well. A part of Grey envied Creton, though, as a couple of Maldon's men dragged his blood and piss-soaked corpse outside to add to the funeral pyre. His war was over. Once the deed was done, in relation to Albret, perhaps then the widower would find some peace too.

13.

Darkness fell like a veil. Stars winked in between ambling clouds.

Amerigo de Pavia, holding a lantern aloft, shifted on the balls of his feet outside the postern gate which he served as captain of. He licked his lips and took a large swig of vinegary wine from the pewter flask he carried. He drank to wet his parched mouth, as well as to try and calm his nerves. In the next hour or so he could either lose his life or gain the greatest sum of money that he had ever laid eyes upon. The receding Lombard had a slight paunch, having eaten well over the Christmas period. He had a plump, pale countenance - and looked like neither a traitor nor hero. Sir Hugh Grey thought de Pavia had an anonymous, forgettable face - which prompted him to think how he might make an effective agent. It seemed he had the mercenary morals to be a spy. He had betrayed the English by entertaining the thought of accepting the French bribe - and then betrayed the French by conspiring with the English. With one hand he carried the lantern, swaying gently in inky night, and with the other he frequently wiped his runny nose.

The captain was accompanied by two men-at-arms, acting as his bodyguards. Gower narrowed his eyes, taking in the half a dozen horsemen cantering towards the walls, and instinctively clasped the sword hanging from his left hip. To the right of de Pavia stood John Wood, a trusted soldier who had fought for years under Sir Walter Manny's banner. The veteran wore an ale-stained jacket over a mail shirt, as well as a rust-spotted helmet. Wood was as coarse as he was courageous, as lewd as he was loyal. He noticed Amerigo shivering, either from the cold or from fear. The craggy-faced soldier from Kent looked to ease the Lombard's mood before the French arrived.

"This will be the last night that you'll ever have to worry about anything again, fella. I understand that you'll be a rich man when all this is over. You'll be able to pluck any wild geese on the streets of Paris. You can have a courtesan rather than common whore hang on your arm, or each arm, from tomorrow."

"I just want to live the quiet life," Amerigo replied, with a faltering or apologetic smile, noticing the increasing tamp of French hooves on the grass beneath his feet.

"Aye, but it takes a lot of money nowadays to be able to afford some peace and quiet in this world," Wood replied, whilst scratching his groin.

Amerigo aimed to appear confident as the French horsemen slowed and stopped. The Lombard puffed out his chest, albeit his stomach still protruded more. He duly noted the large chestnut destrier carrying a sizeable strongbox on its back.

"Are you Amerigo?" Guy Mabrice asked in French, eyeing the three men warily, or accusatory. Even if the angel Gabriel would have accompanied the perfidious English the Frenchman would still not have wholly trusted them. There was too much blood under the bridge between the two countries.

"I am. Are you Mabrice?" the captain of the gate replied.

"I am," the Frenchman asserted, as he stared up at the stone walls looming large before him, thinking how it would take over ten times the number of the forces they had to besiege the port with a chance of success, especially if the walls were manned by English longbowmen.

"I have arranged for a room in the castle where we can talk in private. As I told your commander, I wish to count the first half of my fee before proceeding. I have arranged some refreshments for you and your men too. Come, this way."

"Act like you are participating in a business deal," the English spymaster had advised the Lombard. "Which, in a sense, you are. Look your counterpart in the eye. Be personable and professional. Be eager to collect your bribe. But not too eager.

Gower surveyed the scene in the distance in hope of assessing the extent of de Charny's forces. But it was too dark, and the enemy were still concealing themselves behind the treeline. The man-at-arms also kept his ears open for any loose word one of the French might say, which could provide him with some intelligence.

"And who are you?" Oudart de Renti posed in English, with a sneer, as he passed by John Wood, chewing on a piece of salted pork, thinking how he could have cutdown the man with a couple of strokes of his sword, learned from his fencing masters. It was difficult to know whether the French nobleman had contempt for the soldier because he was English or because he was lowborn. Probably both.

"Just someone who loves coin more than he does his country - and who is tired of taking orders from perfumed pricks like you," John Wood replied, with a snarl.

The tension was as palpable as the chill in the air as the party lowered their heads and made their way through the gate - into the town.

Drunken revellers could be heard in the background, singing their hearts out or unburdening the contents of their stomachs, as the prince, concealed behind a cluster of barrels, spied the handful of French soldiers. His mouth was dry. His palms sweaty. The colour drained from his face as it dawned upon him how much his father was risking. And for what? Sport? Prestige? As much as they had surprise on their side, the French still outnumbered them. There was a danger that de Charny's forces could manage to swarm inside the town and take it.

"The country needs a victory," his father had argued, without confessing that he needed a victory too (although the wishes of king and country were often interchangeable in Edward's eyes). Boredom may have been considered the enemy too, as well as the French. Edward and his eldest son had recently spent a king's ransom, or certainly a princely fortune, at the gambling tables. They had lost in good grace, but lost nevertheless. The prince knew the value of honour, but he was often criticised for not appreciating the value of money. He would lavish gifts upon others and himself (a recent purchase had been a velvet cap, studded with dozens of pearls). Much to his financial adviser's frustration the prince had also written off the debts of many of his tenants in Cheshire, who were struggling to pay their rents due to the pestilence. Money seemed to flow like water through the prince's hands, or like the vintages he added to his wine cellar.

The prince looked on anxiously, worried for his friend as well as for the fate of the kingdom. His tutor, Sir Walter Burley, had schooled the prince in languages, mathematics, rhetoric and lessons in governance. But Gower had taught the young man about how to survive on the battlefield - lessons which would prove more valuable over the coming hours.

Half the town are asleep, the other half are drunk. *Don't give me a great commander, give me a lucky one*, de Charny thought to himself as he watched the giant firefly of the Amerigo's lamp disappear into the town, along with his men. It would be an auspicious beginning to the year if they could take the port back. Ring out the old, ring in the new. If ever France were to invade and conquer the insolent English again, they would need to possess the strategically placed hub. The soldier didn't think he would see in the year in such a way. Indeed, there were times when he considered he would not see in the new year at all, given the ravages of the plague. A year or so ago, just when he believed that they were over the worst of the blight, he realised that the worst had barely reared its ugly head. France could use the win as a tonic for so many of its ills.

Victory at Calais would also help to erase the disappointment and dishonour at being captured during the Battle of Moraix. The crusader wanted, or needed, to redeem himself. The knight gripped the reins in his gauntleted hands, but he knew he had to endure the calm before the storm first. Soldiers, like Christians, had to be patient. *Amerigo had quite a sum of money to count. We could be in for a long night. But all the nights are long this time of year.*

There would be a contingent of his men who were champing at the bit to fight too, as well as those looking forward to sacking and looting the town. *One might as well as try to remove the red from blood, as extract the greed and cruelty from some men's souls*, de Charny mused.

Horses whinnied and swished their tales as the army waited in the woods. In the background de Charny could also hear Charles de Jardun impatiently and annoyingly tap his spurs against his mount. It still may have been the least irritating thing about the man, de Charny told himself. He spoke about the quality of his armour once more. The commander was keen to advance, for more than one reason.

14.

De Pavia led Guy Mabrice and his knights into an empty, nondescript property close to the gatehouse. They trudged up a couple of flights of stairs, with Gower and John Wood bringing up the rear, before entering a room which had been stripped of most of its furniture, aside from a table and chair at the back, next to the crackling fireplace.

The welcome was far from warm though as the French were confronted by several English soldiers, their weapons drawn. Gower and Wood had also unsheathed their blades. They prompted their guests to all enter the room.

"My name is Sir Walter Manny. I am afraid that things have not gone as expected, for you," the knight said with a hint of a smile, witnessing the surprised and less than ebullient expressions on French faces. "I trust that you will surrender peaceably. Enough blood will doubtless be spilled this evening - but let us endeavour to avoid spilling it now."

Sir Walter, originally from Hainault, was fluent in both French and English. Both steeliness and courtesy infused his tone. The nobleman possessed courtly manners but behaved with a different species of etiquette when fighting in the saddle, a broadsword in hand. Striking hazel eyes, which shone like varnished oak, were set within a strong, even countenance. His long hair was parted in the middle and streaked with grey, as if he had just walked through a low-ceilinged room strewn with cobwebs. The Scottish had called the accomplished soldier "a scourge," which he felt suitably proud about. He had originally travelled over from Hainault in the party containing Edward's soon to be wife. The king soon recognised and rewarded his virtues and ambition, becoming a trusted and loyal commander. Sir Walter was now proud to call England his home (despite its recent harrowing). The soldier of fortune had been good to England and England had been good to him. He considered himself devout. The Christian soldier had pleaded with the king to show mercy towards the burghers of Calais at the close of the siege.

Sir Walter displayed less mercy, however, when he stormed a highland stronghold and slaughtered more Scots than he could recall. The knight felt duly honoured when Edward offered him command of the imminent engagement, although he was well aware that his king could revoke his command and take over at any given moment.

A brief silence ensued, aside from the creaking of warped, worn floorboards. The room smelled of sweat and woodsmoke and, on the French side, defeat.

Mabrice swore under his breath, albeit a couple of his companions were more audible in their curses. For a moment he was sorely tempted to draw his sword in the hope of running the traitor through, as much as the Lombard appeared slightly sheepish and ashamed.

"He's sober, but I bet the peacock feels as sick as any sot doubled over in the alley outside," John Wood commented, nodding towards Oudart de Renti. "My cock's got a better colour to it - and doesn't feel as limp either, I warrant."

"Ha!"

Edward couldn't help but be amused the man-at-arms' jibe. He might even reward the soldier with a coin or two. The king sat on the chair at the back of the room, half concealed in the shadows. His arm rested on the table, which would shortly be home to the strongbox. He would often recall a quote by Sir Hugh Grey, from Cicero: "Money is the sinew of war." Although Edward was eager to deposit the bounty into his treasury (minus the fee for de Pavia), the king was even keener to don his armour and spring his trap for de Charny. In a letter to the Lombard the French commander had revealed how his men would signal the French advance by hoisting the French colours up and waving a lantern from the top of the gatehouse.

Although he could not be judged responsible for the mission's failure, Mabrice still felt that he had let his commander - and himself - down. It would prove pointless to try and fight their way out. They would be cut down before they could even draw their weapons.

After surrendering to the English knight, Mabrice glowered at the Lombard. If looks could kill, Gower thought. Unfortunately, for the Frenchman, they didn't.

Sir Walter instructed Sir John Beauchamp to incarcerate the prisoners but treat them well. Oudart de Renti hoped that any chronicles would report that Mabrice, rather than himself, led the calamitous advance party.

The prince and Gower, mounted on their horses, along with the reserve force, watched the Frenchmen being escorted to their makeshift cell. Feet scraped across flagstones. Chins dug into chests. Their heads were bowed in submission, aside from Mabrice's. Beauchamp informed the French knight who the person was commanding the reserve. A shocked Mabrice mustered as determined and challenging gaze as he could - but the prince ignored him, turning his attention towards his friend. The king had suggested that he refrain from wearing his distinctive black armour, to help retain his anonymity. The prince leaned forward and rubbed an ear of his horse. He didn't know why it helped settle the creature, but it worked and the fierce destrier appeared to like it. The prince smiled, as he recalled how an earl's daughter he had deflowered had similarly stroked his ear in bed - and the sensation had soothed him.

"I am heartily glad that you are with us, William. No matter what happens, it won't be as bad as Crécy," the prince asserted.

Both men momentarily twitched or shivered as their inward eyes remembered the great battle. They had been surrounded by growling Frenchmen, caked in mud and blood. Intent on slaughtering any and all Englishmen. A song of steel and death rang around them. The prince had been at the vanguard of the fighting, a target to capture or kill. God knows how he found the strength to keep his sword arm raised.

"Not a lot could be," Gower replied, thinking how at least no one was now carrying the prince's banner, drawing the French towards it like moths to a flame. Believing that it was worth trading freedom of movement for protection, Gower wore a gambeson with a few plates and mail sewn onto the garment, rather than a full suit of armour. He also wore a sallet, so he could better see his surroundings.

"Unfortunately, we may not see much action this evening. We may not even be called upon at all," the prince said, puffing out his cheeks in disgruntlement or frustration.

Gower was less sure as to how unfortunate it would be. More than testing himself against Geoffrey de Charny, he wanted to get back to England and Eleanor with all his limbs - and other vital parts of his person - intact. He needed at least one knee and a hand to propose. The soldier's mouth grew dry - and his heart pounded as powerfully as any war drum - at the thought of asking the woman he loved to be his wife. Strangely, he felt more dread at the prospect of Eleanor saying yes rather than no.

"I couldn't ever imagine waking up to the same woman every day," Owain had expressed earlier in the week. "It's rare that I'll even sleep with the same whore twice."

"If it's any comfort, I can't imagine a woman ever wanting to wake up to you each morning in return, unless she was blind - as well as Welsh," Gower countered in good humour.

The prince was occupied with his own private thoughts, as Gower was his. Certainly, his father would see some combat this evening. He would be eager to engage the French, to the point of perhaps being rash and overextending himself. He would be drawn to de Charny's banner, blinded by rage or glory.

"You have nothing to prove to anyone, father," the prince had argued the previous evening, hoping to temper his desire to ride into the thick of the fighting and engage the French commander.

"We all have something to prove to ourselves - and God - each day. I have not travelled here to be a mere spectator to proceedings."

The prince resolved that he would advance with the reserve when he saw fit, rather than if called upon. The night before he dreamt that he had clashed swords with de Charny. He rode a large, black, snorting warhorse. The knight carried his colours in one hand and a gleaming broadsword in the other, as polished as his fine armour. The prince's shield grew splintered from his opponent's blows and his blade broke in two but still he valiantly or vainly fought on. He woke, drenched in sweat, before the contest was settled.

Clouds parted. Stars glistered.

Geoffrey de Charny took a breath and appeared even more focused, if it were possible, as a light could be seen through the gelid gloom. The lantern shone like a beacon, welcoming a fleet home. The Lombard had proved more faithful than the Genevan crossbowman who had stood (but not for too long) at Crécy.

The drawbridge was being lowered. The portcullis raised. It was time.

CALAIS

A fair few soldiers crossed themselves and kissed crucifixes around their necks. Some muttered or murmured, "Monjoie, Saint Denis," the French battle-cry. One veteran knight, who had fought and been wounded at the fall of Caen, could be heard saying to his squire:

"Fight as if the sacred Oriflamme has been unfurled. Give no quarter."

The commander kicked his heels into the flanks of his horse and set off. In the distance, a mass of troops could be seen advancing towards the Boulogne Gate. Once free of the treeline de Charny took in a lungful of sea air, before lowering his visor. His standard bearer cantered beside him, but the knight quickened his pace still. He wanted to lead from the front - and de Charny didn't want to make a liar of any chronicler who reported that he was the first to enter through the gates of the town.

Hooves tamped upon the turf, spitting up mud. Cries of "Montjoie! Saint Denis!" grew more full-throated. But the French would soon hear the war cry of, "For England and Saint George!"

15.

Dawn would soon breach the horizon, as the French would break through into the town, de Charny thought. He had the numbers, he judged. It would be five thousand of his troops against no more than two thousand English. But the French commander was about to realise that the numbers wouldn't add up. It was always darkest before the dawn.

The French poured over the drawbridge - the moat below the colour of the Acheron - and through the gates, like hounds with the scent of a fox in their nostrils. Night and the dust blurred their vision.

They came through into a large space, where part of the garrison would muster when conducting an inspection. But the space wasn't as empty as de Charny had hoped. The English had constructed false walls, made of dry stone, either side of the gate. Mounted knights and men-at-arms on foot now streamed out from behind the walls to surround their enemy. The trap was sprung. A trumpet blared out. Sir Waler Manny gave the order to tip the large stone, positioned on the top of the gatehouse, onto the drawbridge below, which had been part sawn-through earlier in the day. The boulder crashed through the wooden bridge, barring any reinforcements. Yet still a formidable French force remained inside the town.

"We need some sport, Sir Walter," the king had explained. "It should be a fair fight."

The enemy appeared like startled deer. Like lambs to the slaughter. The distinctive, dreadful sound of bowstrings twanging, succeeded by the swish of arrows, filled the scene as a row of archers unleashed a volley into the attackers. An arrowhead pierced Augustus de Corbie helm and forehead, parting his beloved fringe.

A contingent of longbowmen also rose up upon the battlements and didn't waste any time in emptying their arrow bags into their stranded opponents beneath them. French war cries turned into blood-curdling screams.

"It's like shooting fish in a barrel," one Kentish bowman remarked to his friend, as he nocked another arrow and sent the missile into a retreating French horseman.

"Aye, but fish have stronger spines," the archer replied, his wide grin resembling the shape of his great war bow.

Unfortunately, there was no scope for the invaders inside to retreat. The blood drained from de Charny's handsome face as he realised that he had been betrayed - the victim rather than the author of a subterfuge. His stomach tightened, as no doubt some of his countrymen loosened their bowels. Surrendering would be tantamount to a slaughter. Pride, honour or anger compelled the commander to give the order to fight.

"Form up! Form up! Defensive positions," the knight bellowed, though he couldn't be sure if his words were just one sound getting scattered and lost in the wind.

The hairs on the back of Sir Walter's nape tingled, although the sensation may have been due to feeling of the king breathing down his neck. The knight gave the order to attack, his voice cutting through the air like an executioner's axe.

The mass of men may not have experienced combat for several years, but a fire in their bellies had been ignited. The soldiers still knew the weak points in a suit of armour and knew when to cut and when to thrust. To kill or be killed.

The king was one of the first to engage the enemy, making a beeline for the nearest French knight. Like a lion to the slaughter. Edward swatted his opponent's sword away and punched his shield forward, unseating the rider. He would let one of the unmounted men-at-arms entering the fray capture or end the Frenchman. Fighting wasn't fencing. "The rules of chivalry are written in ink. Those of fighting are written in blood," Edward had, at more than once juncture, explained to his son. Unbeknownst to the king, Sir Walter had instructed a couple of knights to shadow and protect the monarch. What would it profit the kingdom if they retained the town but lost a king? They followed Edward as he cut a furrow into the French, like a plough scything through virgin soil, as he endeavoured to reach de Charny's standard. Should the king have lifted his visor at this point one would have witnessed a man smiling rather than snarling. The fighting reminded him of many a melee that he had participated in at various tournaments. Edward was enjoying being free from the burden of command, being a plain soldier in unmarked armour.

Chaos and carnage took hold, like a dog with a bone. As Sir Roger Mortimer grappled with an opponent, a gout of blood splattered against his chest, as out the corner of his eye an English mace ripped off half a French bascinet - and half a face to boot. Sir Walter Manny told himself that he would refrain from engaging, as he needed to issue orders and assess the overall picture of the unfolding battle. But he couldn't help but roar forward and hack at an enemy when he saw Sir John Beauchamp in peril.

Men-at-arms often hunted in pairs to drag French knights - riding fine horses, clad in fine armour - to the ground. Saving Calais was all well and good - but securing ransom money was even more welcome. One soldier, brandishing a St George's flag, was cut down by a French broadsword, but the banner was quickly picked up and the offending knight was run through using the spear point of the Englishman's falchion. An enraged John Wood stabbed the belly of a chestnut palfrey. The horse shrieked, reared up and threw its rider. The man-at-arms lost little time, or remorse, in stabbing his prostrate enemy in the neck.

"Do you hear that, William?" the prince said, leaning forward in his saddle, his horse scraping the ground, seemingly as eager as his owner to enter the contest.

"No. What do you hear?"

"The signal to advance."

Gower half-smiled.

"I hear it now," the man-at-arms responded, registering no such sound, before turning to give the order for the reserves to advance.

Cheers rang out from the battlements as archers celebrated seeing off the frustrated French army, which had been cut off from their commander and comrades inside the town. Corpses and horses littered the ground, like a trail of detritus, as the French retreated even faster than they had advanced. A few longbowmen still chanced their arm at shooting at the far-off, fleeing soldiers, but their work was done. Some cursed the absence of the drawbridge, as they wouldn't be able to expediently venture out and loot the dead and dying.

Geoffrey de Charny fought valiantly but many of his soldiers were not equal to his efforts, and his forces were whittled down. The rousing battle cries became drowned out by death rattles. The French commander had no time to direct his troops either, as he found himself fighting for his life at the heart of the melee. He noticed how one determined Englishman had cut a swathe through his men in an effort to engage him.

They traded blows. Their arms ached and sweat stung their eyes - but they kept their swords and shields raised. Sometimes skilfully. Sometimes desperately. Jostling. Hacking. They were well-matched. De Charny wondered, as he fended off another attack with his battered shield, who his opponent might be. Had he gained fame in tournaments? Was he an English nobleman? He might have even admired his opponent, if he did not want to defeat him so much. The king bared his teeth and swore beneath his visor. He was indeed being tested, to the point of being bested. The stalemate ended through the intervention of an English man-at-arms pulling the Frenchman from his great warhorse. De Charny found himself winded, helpless, on his back. A second man-at-arms stood over the French knight, wielding a bloody double-bladed axe. He raised the weapon above his head, with the intention of delivering a fatal blow. But a sword was thrust forward, deflecting the attack. Sparing the Frenchman.

"We're not in the habit of executing enemy commanders. God knows we're barbaric enough," the king remarked, after lifting his visor. "You have fought well, soldier. Take this man and deliver him to Sir Walter Manny. Treat him with due courtesy and honour."

The moment proved somewhat of a blur to de Charny, who squinted in the gloom, his visor raised, as the lives and the surcoats of the French noblemen lay in tatters around him.

"It wasn't supposed to turn out this way," the French commander asserted, either to himself or the Englishman. His armour and spirits crumpled.

"It is as it is," Edward replied, without rancour.

16.

A murky, tawny light seeped across the horizon, like blood oozing from a wound.

The battle was seemingly over. The French - those who could still draw breath - surrendered. Defeat and despondency were etched into features, like words chiselled into tombstones. A young knight from Rheims lay crushed beneath his horse, his pelvis shattered, as he called out for God to save him. He didn't answer. Sir Walter Manny almost felt sorry for Geoffrey de Charny as he gave him back his sword and accepted his surrender. Almost, but not quite.

The king's blood was up, however. A taste of glory fed rather than satisfied his appetite. After hearing that the remnants of a second force were still congregating outside the Boulogne Gate, Edward commanded his household cavalry and a group of nearby archers to follow him.

"There's more sport to be had!"

Most had fled. Their commander had failed to open the gate. Yet some were still loyal, or foolish, enough to believe that de Charny would take the gatehouse. Shields were raised as arrows spat down upon them from the couple of dozen archers manning the walls. Every now and then a crossbow quarrel would clatter against the crenelated battlements in reply.

The black, iron portcullis was finally cranked open. But instead of witnessing their brothers-in-arms pour forth a torrent of English horsemen appeared. Edward spurred his mount and men on, an Achilles commanding his Myrmidons. Or King Arthur leading the Knights of the Round Table. The French knew that something had gone wrong with de Charny's assault. They wheeled their horses around, retreating down the causeway. The stragglers were cut down - lances, swords and maces scything through armour and flesh. A mounted man-at-arms who had joined the pack sliced through the hamstring of a French mare, slowing the beast, whilst a member of the king's household guard then slashed his sword across the rider's neck. Blood freckled the grass, like morning dew.

CALAIS

Archers breathlessly followed the English cavalry through the gate, in the pursuit of coin more than glory. The bowmen did not take long to realise, however, that they may have bitten off more than they could chew.

It also dawned upon Bernard Clermont, the commander of the French secondary force, that the English had made an error in judgement. The knight, a competent soldier, was not without courage - and not against winning a semblance of honour back. Clermont was pockmarked, with a pronounced downturned mouth. He had suffered the strange distinction of losing both of his little fingers, having had them severed in two different battles. A fog of failure hung over him as his forces were compelled to retreat - but the fog suddenly began to clear. His mouth was even upturned in something resembling a smile - as he turned to survey the scene. The English attackers could be numbered in their tens. The French were several hundred men strong. The English knight leading their charge was brave, but foolhardy. He had made an error of judgement - a potentially fatal mistake.

Clermont rallied his men:

"Look! See! The arrogant enemy have overextended themselves. They are few. We are many. Punish the perfidious English!"

Hubris drove Edward on, sweat beading his brow. The king was overestimating the strength of his numbers and underestimating the enemy's resolve. The French were not completely broken. They were re-forming and advancing.

"Damn them!" the king said to himself, conscious that it might now be himself who was damned. The ground shook from the enemy horses eating up the distance between the two sides. Edward turned around. The archers had slowed to a standstill. Doubt afflicted the countenances of his household cavalry. English resolve was close to breaking, as they observed the French - and defeat - on the horizon.

The king deftly wheeled his destrier around, lifted his visor, and addressed his soldiers, his voice reverberating like thunder, as sharp and unyielding as the great blade he carried.

"Bowmen of England. Your king needs you. I am Edward of Windsor - shoot for me!"

Some of the soldiers recognised the voice and figure of their sovereign, having served with him before. As initially astounded as the archers were, they no longer harboured any thoughts of retreating. Their barrel chests swelled even more, with pride or bellicosity. They moved forward as one and reached into their arrow bags. They had no need of a captain to instruct them to nock, aim, loose. Missiles arced over Edward's head and buried themselves into the enemy. The bowmen started to thin the enemy's numbers and slow their charge but the bulk of Clermont's troops inexorably advanced.

For a moment Edward paused and regretted that he had not taken confession that morning. He thought how he should have also composed a letter to his wife. The king loved his queen dearly, despite his infidelities. He thought how he had taught his son much to prepare him for his future. But there was still much for him to learn. He felt like there was a hole inside him, as big as a grave. Edward always imagined that he would die a wise, old king. He fancied that he would, on his deathbed, quote Augustus Caesar: "Have I played my part well?"

Inspired by the archer's actions, Edward's household guard rallied to their king. They would have created a ring if steel, if not for their commander insisting on fighting by their side.

A clash of arms erupted in the half-light. A flurry of blades danced in the air. Blows and insults were traded. Gore soon stained armour and trappings alike. Edward parried a sword blow with one hand whilst holding his shield aloft to block another. An unmounted French man-at-arms suddenly appeared in front him, brandishing an axe. Edward made a special click with his tongue and his horse reared up on two legs, its flailing front hooves stoving in the enemy's skull. A few arrows still zipped in the background, picking off the French on the flanks who were looking to wrap around the English and envelop them.

God be with me, Edward thought - either hoping that the Almighty would come to his aid or be with him at his death, as the soldier feared judgement.

The English battled on. The French - and death - were drawing in as if Edward were Jonah and the whale was closing its jaws. He saw a lance pierce one of his men. His tongue lolled out the side of his mouth, akin to a dog. A mace struck the king's shoulder. Although it failed to pierce his armour the blow was enough to disorientate him. Clermont was close by and decided to blindside his enemy. The Frenchman pulled his arm back in preparation to thrust his sword into the English commander when a horse careered into his own. It was Clermont's turn to be disorientated. The prince, in one fluid movement, drew his sword and back slashed against his opponent, severing more than just a finger.

The prince and Gower were at the spear tip of the contingent of reserves who had pursued the king, after learning of his sally out of the Boulogne Gate. Both men were unsure whether they had ever ridden as hard.

If God was on his side, the presence of his son was just as welcome.

Gower sided up to the king too, on the opposite side to the prince, and hacked away at a French knight, disarming him - before punching his shield forward and unseating the enemy. The attack wasn't elegant, but it was effective. The man-at-arms proceeded to turn to his next opponent. And turn his opponent into a victim, as Gower thrust the point of his sword upwards into the Frenchman's unprotected chin, skewering his brain.

The prince's reserves caught up and joined the fray, pushing back the tide of steel and flesh. But a fresh wave of French infantry and cavalry were about to advance, observing how the battle hung in the balance. There were spoils to be won. Both the king and prince realised that if the enemy reserves circled around the rear of their meagre force, then they were as good as dead. Calais falling might have caused them less distress. Gower fought on, furiously, butting an opponent before jabbing his sword through the man's mail, as he also kicked a nearby infantryman. But the oncoming enemy gave him pause. His stomach churned, his Adam's apple bobbed up and down. The soldier regretted not having already asked Eleanor to marry him.

The ground shook even more, as if it were about to open-up and bury them in a mass grave.

But it was the French who suddenly needed to protect their rear as the awful, familiar sound of a volley of English arrows hissed through the air. Maldon's company of archers had dismounted and formed up. The tired soldiers, weary from travelling through the cold night, came back to life. Springs uncoiling.

"Shoot at will. Cut the bastards down," Richard Maldon had ordered, whilst reaching for his own bow. Every missile could count.

Owain was perhaps the first to unleash an arrow. As much as the king was in danger, as Grey warned, the Welshman thought he spied his friend in the thick of the fight.

Broadhead and bodkin-tipped arrows thumped into backs and the haunches of mounts. Soldiers sometimes fell, sometimes slumped off their horses. A few were briefly dragged along the ground - their feet caught in the stirrups. Murdered. Mangled. Necks and spines cracking, in an unholy chorus of sounds. There were now too many archers. Too many arrows.

The advance turned into a retreat, as the enemy veered away from the melee and storm of missiles. Maldon ordered half his men to concentrate their efforts of the enemy engaging the king and his forces, trusting that they would hit their marks and strike a foe rather than friend.

The French row was now being attacked from the front and behind. Gower and the prince put themselves in front of the king and broke through the line, with fresh troops following in their wake. The man-at-arms' blade was chipped, his shield disintegrating, but still he hacked and thrusted his way forward. He wasn't fighting to save Calais, he was fighting to protect his friend and his father. Many might have deemed that the soldier was caught in a mad rage, but there was method in his madness. He anticipated the moves of his opponents - or moved so quickly that they did not have time to form a strategy to prepare themselves.

More and more French troops peeled away. Clermont was slain. There was no one to rally them. They hoped that their backs would not become a home to an English missile as they retreated. Some tripped over their own legs, some tripped over the legs of corpses.

Maldon worried that they would soon be out of arrows. But the battle was over. The battle was won.

The king was either too exhausted, or he had learned his lesson in overextending himself, to pursue the enemy.

"Let them flee, all the way back to Paris. They can deliver the news to Philip that this is still English soil."

CALAIS

Few men cheered in the aftermath, but partly because they were breathless.

Enough blood had been spilled. Sufficient glory had been won. The chroniclers had their story. It had been a near run thing. Edward beamed with pride at his blood-stained son, tears pricking his eyes - which he swiftly and discretely wiped away. The prince had fought with skill and valour. His men had fought for him too. Perhaps he was ready for his own command and campaign. Or there was no perhaps about it.

"I'm getting tired of saving your life," Maldon remarked to Gower, as the two friends clasped one another on the shoulder.

"I'm not," the man-at-arms drolly replied, his breath misting up the morning air, which began to reek of death and horseshit.

Flies commenced to congregate over the slain and dying. Bowmen scurried around too. Throats were slit, purses cut open, fingers hacked off to retrieve rings. A few of the enemy were spared, as their fine armour bespoke of a soul worth saving - and ransoming.

"I couldn't be pleased to see you more, even if you were carrying a choice vintage with you, Sir Hugh," the king said to his spymaster.

"You underestimate my wine cellar. We both have cause to celebrate, it seems. Suffice to say that Raymon Creton can only spread his lies and build a network of agents in hell now. I'm grateful for the loan of Maldon's company. They performed admirably."

"I am grateful in return for you lending us your man-at-arms. I am here by the grace of God - and his intervention. I may have use for such a soldier in the future."

"I would you grant him some time to recover. William is about to engage on the most arduous campaign of his life. He is getting married."

The dawn's rosy fingertips clawed their way up into the sky. Sir Walter Manny rode out to report to his king:

"The prisoners are secure. I have given Sir Geoffrey my own quarters... The butcher's bill on our side could have been much worse. The surgeons are tending to the wounded. Priests are attending to the dying."

"Thank you, Sir Walter. You fought and led well. I could not have done better myself," Edward expressed, with warmth and respect. The compliment may have been the greatest in all Christendom, Sir Hugh Grey wryly thought to himself.

17.
Epilogue.

The following evening.

It was a feast fit for a king, which was apt. Long, oak tables were laden with roasted meats (pork, partridge, chicken, wood pigeon, venison), steaming vegetables (radishes, turnips, skirret, spinach, lovage) and desserts (honey cakes, fruit, sweet pastries).

"The courses keep coming, like the waves of cavalry at Crécy," one guest proffered, as his breeches began to bite into his burgeoning hips. Later in the evening, out of embarrassment and contrition, he would gift the whore a few extra coins for being sick over her.

The Knights of the Garter were present, along with other noblemen and the distinguished French prisoners the English were playing host to. The king considered Sir Geoffrey de Charny an honoured guest. Initially, Edward gently chided and mocked the Frenchman:

"The subterfuge was beneath a commander of your standing. Perhaps Philip will permit you the honour of facing us in a pitched battle next time. You sought to buy cheaply what I had earned at great expense."

But the two soldiers duly warmed to one another. It was important to be gracious, in defeat or victory.

"You must dine with me tomorrow, too, Sir Geoffrey. I would much like to discuss the tenets of Vegetius with you - and gossip about the beauties and bastards in the French court."

"It will be another long dinner then," the knight replied, thinking how he was starting to enjoy the company of the English king more than his own monarch.

De Charny noted how Edward took time out to speak to his prisoners with reverence and kindness. The knight was also suitably touched by the king's son personally serving him at dinner. The Frenchman was impressed by the prince's courteousness, as well as courage. He was his father's son. Although the commander did not resent his host for having bested him, the Christian soldier could not forgive the treacherous Lombard - and swore vengeance on the absent de Pavia.

"This will not be the end of his story. No. The Lombard's ending will not be a happy one," de Charny vowed to Mabrice later in the night.

For most of the banquet Guy Mabrice sat, sullen, in the corner. As much as he drank, the wine could not wash away the bitter taste of defeat. He often glared at the English prince, stewing in resentment. He felt a pang of envy when his commander smiled during their conversation - and his mentor graciously bowed to him. Mabrice vowed that he would endeavour to face the prince in a tournament one day, or better still on the battlefield.

What little fame and regard he will have left will die with him.

The prince was oblivious to the French soldier's animus. His muscles ached, despite the copious amount of wine he consumed to deaden the pain. Or rather his joints may have been stiff from having paid a visit to Maggie Tunbridge that afternoon. It was difficult to know which one of them had taken advantage of the other more.

There was a musical interlude of a harpist and chorister during the banquet. A priest also said a few words for the fallen. Edward felt blessed by God for having survived another battle, but he felt less blessed for having to endure the clergyman drone on for longer than necessary. In a few quiet, private moments Edward could be seen to wince in discomfort. His shoulder smarted and his torso was riddled with bruises. He felt more than one blister burst on his feet as he visited every corner of the room. The king was only too pleased to host and honour his chivalrous prisoner, but part of him yearned to travel back home. He wanted to see his wife - and mistresses - again. There was much to attend to in his kingdom too, which resembled an un-weeded garden in places.

The wine and conversation flowed. Few spoke about the pestilence. Toasts were made and cups re-filled. More logs were tossed on the fires to fuel the warm atmosphere. The celebratory mood seemed not just a release in relation to the past couple of days, but the past couple of years too.

Many an English knight recounted the recent battle, from their point of view. They polished their stories, as much as their squires were currently buffing their armour. Everyone deserved to have a troubadour sing a song devoted to their exploits. More wine was found to lubricate the festivities, though the king was also mindful to make sure that the townspeople had enough drink and victuals to partake in the victory celebrations as well. Alas, Tom Rudge and his guild were still suffering from sore heads for a different reason - and were unable to participate.

William Gower appeared a mite ill at ease and refrained from wholly throwing himself into the celebrations. The king had invited the commoner to sit alongside him at the top table, which didn't quite entirely endear the man-at-arms to a number of English noblemen. But Edward rightly toasted the soldier during dinner:

"This man, along with my goodly son, saved my life. I think that entitles him to sit at this table… William fought like a lion," Edward announced, with Gower looking somewhat sheepish in response. There was part of the common soldier which wanted to excuse himself from the august gathering and join Owain and Maldon at The Rusty Nail. He preferred sitting on a bench with an ale, to sitting with the Knights of the Garter drinking fine wines.

Sir Hugh Grey smiled into his winecup, amused by his friend's reaction. He probably would have favoured being at the heart of a melee right now, surrounded by enemies baying for his blood, to being the centre of attention at such a banquet.

"You are right to be worried, William. You have caught the attention of the king and made a name for yourself. Such notoriety can prove a curse and a blessing. You may be able to name your price, should you be asked to serve under the king's banner. But you have also realised the value of a peaceful existence and the love of a good woman," Grey remarked. It was the nobleman's turn to appear a little uneasy, albeit briefly, as he remembered Grace and he felt a pang of grief, as if a cutpurse had just stabbed him in between the ribs with a stiletto blade.

"I am going to ask Eleanor to marry me," Gower declared, after a moment's pause, with as much diffidence as delight in his voice.

"I know."

"How do you know?"

"I'm a spy. It's my job to know things, especially secrets. I also know that she will accept your proposal. There is no need to fret, William. Marriage will suit you."

"How so?"

"Because you're a soldier - and married life is a constant battle."

The two men grinned, clinked cups and downed their wine.

End Note.

Calais: Men-At-Arms is a work of fiction. As a novelist I get to make stuff up. The details surrounding the subterfuge and battle for the town are also far from clear and agreed upon.

My hope is that this novella has stirred your interest into knowing more about the real history behind the historical fiction. For those wishing to read about Edward of Woodstock there is *The Black Prince*, by Michael Jones. For those interested in Edward III there is *The Perfect King*, by Ian Mortimer. For a general history of The Hundred Years War, I can recommend *A Great and Glorious Adventure*, by Gordon Corrigan. Helen Carr has also recently published an engaging and insightful history of the 14th century, *Sceptred Isle*. Should you wish to depress yourself and read about the Black Death then there's *The Great Mortality*, by John Kelly. If you are interested in reading more fiction set during the Hundred Years War then I can recommend *The Grail Quest* by Bernard Cornwell, as well as the *Essex Dogs* books by Dan Jones. Should you have enjoyed the Men-At-Arms series then you may want to try the *Band of Brothers* books, set during Henry V's Agincourt campaign.

Do please get in touch should you have enjoyed any of my titles. I can be reached via richard@sharpebooks.com or on twitter @rforemanauthor

William Gower and Sir Hugh Grey will return in *Poitiers: Men-At-Arms*.

Richard Foreman.

Printed in Dunstable, United Kingdom